NAPOLEON HILL's
Putting the Principles into Practice

Giving Every Child a Legacy for Life

by
Napoleon Hill & Judith Williamson

Children's Stories by
Havilah Malone & Diane Lampe
Illustrations by Youjin Oh

A Publication of
THE NAPOLEON HILL FOUNDATION

NAPOLEON HILL's
Putting the Principles into Practice

Giving Every Child a Legacy for Life

Copyright 2015 The Napoleon Hill Foundation

All rights reserved, including the right to reproduce, transmit, store, perform or record the contents hereof.

Published by:

> The Napoleon Hill Foundation
> P.O. Box 1277
> Wise, Virginia USA 24293
> Website: www.naphill.org
> Email: napoleonhill@uvawise.edu

> Napoleon Hill World Learning Center
> Purdue University Calumet
> 2300 173rd Street
> Hammond, Indiana 46323
> Email: nhf@purduecal.edu

Written by Napoleon Hill with contemporary commentary by Judith Williamson, Director, Napoleon Hill World Learning Center

PUTTING THE PRINCIPLES INTO PRACTICE

ISBN: 978-1-937641-99-3

*Dedicated to the Teacher in all of us
who wants to make the world a better
place for all the children of the world today.*

Foreword

Dear Parents, Relatives, Teachers, Mentors, and Friends,

Other than food, shelter, and clothing, reading is the very next best thing that you can do for your children to prepare them for their future. Not only does reading enrich the mind but it helps young personalities grow and bloom into a sense of purpose with an understanding of what life is about.

Readers are truly leaders in all walks of life, and the gift of reading is a legacy for a lifetime. How do I know this? I am certain of these facts by the way my mother cultivated reading in my development and gave me the gift of having an infinite number of teachers in books and stories. I was not place bound because of where I lived. From my early years I traveled and learned about new people, countries, and cultures through books. I read biographies, learned about saints and sinners, and enjoyed silly stories as one of my favorite pastimes through reading.

I read out loud, to my mother, to my dolls, and even to my cats if they were a willing audience. But in fact, all the time, I was reading to and for myself. Today, I am certified as a reading professional K-12 and hold a license to develop a school reading program that advances through the grade levels. I can also work to diagnose reading problems in individuals. But, that is not what I choose to do now. Instead, I choose to instill the value of reading in people through my authorship of writings aligned with Napoleon Hill's works.

I see a void between young people of today and those from decades ago. Reading needs to be introduced and "massaged" into our children so that they will know where to turn for help and feel good about the process. Scientists, psychologists, and every reader knows the intrinsic value of reading in introducing children to life's values and beliefs that help sustain them into adulthood and even old age.

Reading is an elixir, a fountain of youth, a trophy that is a passageway to the very best future that you can gift a child. But, the books read need to be quality readings. They need to inspire mind work like imagination, creativity, dedication, discipline, and self-care that will create pathways in the brain that exceed what happens without reading.

In a study of elderly nuns' ongoing brain capacity, it was recently found that those nuns who read from an early age were less inclined to display symptoms of Alzheimer's disease in their senior years, even if they were genetically predisposed and were expected to display the symptoms. Why? Because through reading, new neurological pathways were created early on in the brain that gave them alternative methods to think and respond when old pathways were mangled or destroyed.

In the book entitled *Aging With Grace* that shares findings from the Nun Study, author David Snowdon, Ph.D. quotes Dr. Susan Kemper, a psycholinguist who studies the impact of aging on language skills. Dr. Kemper states adamantly that "the best way to increase vocabulary and reading comprehension is by starting early in life, by reading to your children." This one action, reading to children, is powerful and can increase the brain's growth and activity throughout a person's lifetime. The simple answer unequivocally is to read to children which in turn aids in the creation of multiple connections between nerve cells. This simple activity works to enhance our brain capacity.

Reading is like brain insurance. Reading is like the magical potion that can assist us in sustaining our brain functions well into our 80's and 90's. Remember this significant fact. This only works if children have been read to and became readers themselves at an early age. Truly, reading widens our horizons and cultivates texture and richness in our daily lives and later experiences as an adult.

By beginning with this book of examples and suggestions,

you can introduce your child to reading for pleasure and purpose. If at first you express joy in reading, and model this behavior often at home your child will too. By reading daily you catch the attention of your child at a young age and they imprint your behavior and want to do what you are doing. Reading is contagious and something very good to catch. No vaccine required.

Reading suggestions in this book are my personal choices and examples. They correspond to the principles that Dr. Napoleon Hill teaches for a lifetime of richness and success in many ways. If you go to the library, purchase a book, read it online, or find it elsewhere, you will benefit your children immensely.

By reading the children's rhymed stories written by Havilah Malone and Diane Lampe, you will be giving your child an appetizer that encourages them to find hidden nutrition in stories that can feed them for life. All it takes is a little effort on your part, or the part of a relative or mentor, who wants to introduce children to the joys and benefits of reading. Whether you read for fun, for education, for armchair traveling, for a release from the ordinary, or to cultivate your imagination and creativity, to learn how people lived astounding lives, or just to pass time, reading contains something for everyone.

Reading is a gift that literally lasts a lifetime, keeps on giving, and grows a brain full of beauty and richness. Particulars aside, reading is a fun and valuable activity that allows each and every one of us to become the person we envision becoming.

Fail to read. Fail to succeed. It is as simple and complex as that. Readers are leaders. If you want to be one, get out those books and learn the lessons of your choice.

Happy Reading!
Be Your Very Best Always through READING!
Judith Williamson

PRINCIPLE 1

Definiteness of Purpose

Definiteness of Purpose is the starting point of all achievement. All individual achievement begins with the adoption of a definite major purpose and a specific plan for its attainment. Without a purpose and a plan, people drift aimlessly throughout life. Lack of Definiteness of Purpose is the greatest stumbling block to 98 out of every 100 persons because they never really define their goals and start toward them with Definiteness of Purpose. Ideas form the foundation of all fortunes and the starting point of all inventions. Once a student learns how to harness the power of his mind and then how to organize the knowledge, he begins to keep his mind on the things he wants and off the things he does not want.

CHAPTER 1

If people are our greatest resource then it goes without saying that children are our greatest future resource. Holding that thought, it makes sense to instruct children in ways and manners in their upbringing that contribute to the betterment of their lives now and in the future. With children, it is best to begin at the beginning, so this book, ***Putting the Principles into Practice,*** will be dedicated to relating personally selected and reviewed children's stories to the basic message held in each of Napoleon Hill's 17 Success Principles.

In each chapter,
1) A cultural proverb, quote, or saying will be presented along with a discussion connecting its message to one of the success principles.
2) Next, a children's story will be reviewed and showcased for consideration.
3) Finally, a teaching by Dr. Hill will be brought into the discussion for further clarification and study.

These lessons, intended for the young learner, are the link between the story and Dr. Hill's message. The instructional tool of "tell a story make a point," applies here in such a manner that when the child hears or remembers the story he or she will also remember the story's deeper message. Three selected stories will be dedicated to each principle. With this growing anthology of stories and embedded lessons, the young student will begin to understand the fundamental building blocks of Dr. Hill's philosophy—one children's story at a time. By the end of the book, 52 hand selected stories will comprise the instructional anthology for an early success start-up, or success primer for everyone's children.

Let's begin at the beginning...now...Are you ready for a story?

Judith Williamson

Success START-UP! Definiteness of Purpose

*In the end,
We will conserve
only what we love,*

*We will love
only what we understand,*

*We will understand
only what we are taught.*
—BABA DIOUM,
Senegalese
Conservationist

The first principle of success is Dr. Hill's Definiteness of Purpose. This one principle is the key or touchstone in life that enables everything coming next to fall into place. It is the master key that opens doors to our future and aids us in uncovering our purpose as well as our destiny in this life. Life is like a wheel that goes round and round and the still or stationary part of that wheel is the hub which can be a symbol for a small quiet and unchanging internal self.

Each of us holds that unchanging still center in our being and it is who we are—who we enter this world as—with our interior likes and desires that need to be followed for our fulfillment. Each of us is unique, different, and destined to fulfill our life by remembering the internal spark of who we are —our pathway to our internal greatness. Life may be looked upon as a script, our actions the play, and the outcomes our reviews—good or bad. Our script contains the "theme" or purpose that we are born with coupled with our unique spiritual, mental, and physical authorship in making it happen.

Our life's purpose played out on the stage of our life enables us to fulfill the destiny that was only a thought, a seedling, a very tiny sensation or feeling as to who we are and why we are here on this planet. As our seed of thought takes hold in our person, we develop our personality, and grow toward that magnificent obsession that can develop and mature from that one very small and sacred start that Infinite Intelligence placed inside each of us with our personalized DNA. When time is taken to uncover who we really are, or remember who we really are, the next step in creating the life we are meant to live is easy because we are drawn toward our purpose just as many animals are drawn home to their place of origin. Let's consider our first story.

"What is My Song?" by Dennis Linn, Sheila Fabricant Linn and Matthew Linn SJ. Illustrated by Francisco Miranda.

Inside the cover jacket, the book's story is detailed as follows: *Based upon a traditional African fable,* **What is My Song?** *is a story about how every child comes into this world knowing his or her own song or special purpose in life. The book includes a section for parents and caregivers who want to help children stay in touch with their own song.*

Added on the back cover jacket is the following: *Each of us comes into this world for a special reason, with a song that only we can sing. Children know this. Parents who are listening (including adoptive parents and other caring adults) will often hear something of their child's song before the child is born. We don't need to teach our children their special purpose in life, as we would teach them to read or ride a bike. Rather, we need to help them remember what they already know.*

Our special purpose in life—our definite major purpose—is something we come into the world with, remember over time, and use to animate every action in our life that is worthy and honors our innate mission. Sometimes we forget our song, so family, friends and others are often here to help us remember. If we close our eyes, be still, reflect, and listen for our mission in life or our life's song, we will remember it however faintly at first, and more intensely later, because it is who we are from our very beginning.

Note that each book is only showcased in honoring the

authors' copyrighted materials. If you would like to find the book, ask your local librarian to order it for the children's section, or search on Amazon or e-bay for the book, and read it or purchase it for your children's collection.

Remember, "We do not inherit the Earth from our Ancestors; we borrow it from our children." —CHIEF SEATTLE

Each child deserves a fresh beginning and a new start in life.

✦✦✦✦✦✦✦✦✦✦✦✦✦✦✦✦✦✦✦✦✦

The Power of Great Dreams
by Napoleon Hill

Finding your song is much like finding your definite major purpose in life. There are as many songs as there are dreams to be had, but it is crucial that we help children locate the exact, right one. Otherwise, as dreamers often do, they could be chasing shooting starts, when instead their feet should be firmly planted on the ground of their desired purpose. Helping children know their purpose takes our time and talent because little ones not only need guidance but they need to remember the source from which they came and why they were sent. Reflecting early on their purpose by helping them uncover specialized talents and likes and dislikes helps them focus on a life's purpose that can be both joyous and fulfilling rather than just a job that brings them income with no heart.
— Judith Williamson

We who are in this race for riches should be encouraged to know that this changed world in which we live is demanding new ideas, new ways of doing things, new leaders, new inventions, new methods of teaching, new methods of marketing, new books, new literature, new features for television, new ideas for moving pictures. Back of all this demand for new and better things, there is one quality which one must possess to win, and that is *definiteness of purpose,* the knowledge of what one wants, and a burning *desire* to possess it.

We who desire to accumulate riches should remember the real leaders of the world always have been men who harnessed, and put into practical use, the intangible, unseen forces of unborn opportunity, and have converted those forces (or impulses of thoughts) into skyscrapers, cities, factories, airplanes, automobiles, and every form of convenience that makes life more pleasant.

In planning to acquire your share of the riches, let no one influence you to scorn the dreamer. To win the big stakes in this changed world, you must catch the spirit of the great pioneers of the past, whose dreams have given to civilization all that it has of value, the spirit which serves as the life-blood to our own country—your opportunity and mine, to develop and market our talents.

If the thing you wish to do is right and *you believe in it,* go ahead and do it! Put your dream across, and never mind what "they" say if you meet with temporary defeat, for "they," perhaps, do not know that every failure brings with it the seed of an equivalent success.

Source: ***Think and Grow Rich.*** Random House. Trade Edition. 1996. Pgs. 37-38.

CHAPTER 2

*Magic is believing in yourself, if you can
do that, you can make anything happen.*
—JOHANN WOLGANG von GOETHE

In determining our definite major purpose in life, mentors often come into play. Whether these are parents, family members, friends, teachers, ministers or pastors, their commentary and teachings heard by or directed to us often enable us to choose better in life. Children brought up in homes without inspirational nudges often accept their lot in life because they are unaware of what else is available to them in the world. When someone or something comes along to nudge youngsters to a higher level of desire for the good things in life, this is often a turning point in their development. Made to understand that it is not necessary to merely accept what has been given to them but rather to aspire to greatness, the mental light is turned on and the child is never the same. Literally and figuratively "seeing the light" makes a great difference in the outcome of many lives.

Most often it takes a person in the form of a parent, teacher, mentor, or coach who senses that things can change to approach the child and show them a future rich in potential and providing a better lifestyle than they may have been given at birth. There is no sin in striving to be a better person, nor is there anything wrong or unholy in wanting the good things that life has to offer all her children. Sometimes, just by having their awareness raised, children become inspired and enthusiastic about aspiring for more. It could be more education, more friends, more opportunities to create a lifestyle different from what they have now, and more opportunity to embrace the expansive life that the Creator has gifted us with at birth.

This week, I would like to showcase the children's book *"Follow the Moon"* by Sarah Weeks and illustrated by Suzanne Duranceau. This little story involves a boy and a newly hatched sea turtle. On the back cover the author states: *"A newly hatched sea turtle, whose instinct is to 'follow the moon' to find the ocean, is drawn instead by a glittering mirrored ball in a crowded dance club. He is rescued by a young boy who helps him learn to listen to the voice inside his head."* This story uses the young boy as the turtle's mentor. When the turtle makes a mistake and proceeds in the wrong direction, the boy states: *"Turn around, turn around, / That's not the moon you've found."*

Most of us have headed in the wrong direction more than once in our lives. When we have been tapped on the shoulder and reminded to "turn around" because we were approaching a wrong destination someone saw that our path needed to be corrected. As youngsters listen to this story, they understand that it is okay to make corrections and change paths for better outcomes. By listening to someone who may have more experience or knowledge than he or she does, better consequences can follow.

As a youngster, Oliver Napoleon Hill listened to the speech his stepmother gave on that auspicious day in his life regarding poverty. Immediately thereafter his life began to change for the better. So too can we as seasoned adults instruct children to be similarly inspired through Dr. Hill's teachings. Poverty is destructive, but so too are other things in life. Everyone needs to be guided to their true and noble purpose that is placed inside them at birth. That still, small voice within that resonates throughout our life and serves as our internal GPS is what can be compared to be our moon or north star. Just by helping children understand that we can and should seek our definiteness of purpose in life is the entire lesson that is needed to begin the journey from poverty to a lifetime of riches.

✦✦✦✦✦✦✦✦✦✦✦✦✦✦✦✦✦✦✦✦

Experience the Miracle of Life: Master Poverty
by Napoleon Hill

When I was a small boy I heard a very dramatic speech on the subject of poverty which made a lasting impression upon my mind, and I am sure that speech was responsible for my determination to master poverty despite the fact that I had been born in poverty and had never known anything except poverty. The speech came from my stepmother shortly after she came to our home and took over one of the most forlorn, poverty-stricken places I have ever known.

The speech was as follows:
"This place which we call home is a disgrace to all of us and a handicap for our children. We are all able-bodied people and there is no need for us to accept poverty when we know that it is the result of nothing but laziness or indifference.

"If we stay here and accept the conditions under which we now live, our children will grow up and accept these conditions also. I do not like poverty; I have never accepted poverty as my lot, and I shall not accept it now!

"For the moment I do not know what our first step will be in our break for freedom from poverty, but this much I do know—we shall make that break successfully, no matter how long it may take or how many sacrifices we may have to make. I intend that our children shall have the advantage of good educations, *but more than this, I intend that they shall be inspired with the ambition to master poverty.*

"Poverty is a disease which, once it is accepted, becomes a fixation which is hard to shake off.

"It is no disgrace to be born in poverty but it most decidedly is a disgrace to accept this birthright as irrevocable.

"We live in the richest and the greatest country civilization has yet produced. Here opportunity beckons to everyone who has the ambition to recognize and embrace it, and as far as this family is concerned, if opportunity does not beckon to us, *we shall create our own opportunity to escape this sort of life.*

"Poverty is like creeping paralysis! Slowly it destroys the desire for freedom, strips one of the ambition to enjoy better things of life, and undermines personal initiative. Also, it conditions one's mind for the acceptance of myriad fears, including the fear of ill health, the fear of criticism and the fear of physical pain.

"Our children are too young to know the dangers of accepting poverty as their lot, but I shall see to it that they are made conscious of these dangers, and I shall see to it also that they become prosperity conscious, *that they expect prosperity and become willing to pay the price of prosperity.*"

I have quoted this speech from memory, but it is substantially what my stepmother said to my father in my presence shortly after they were married. That "first step" in the break from poverty, which she mentioned in her speech, came when my stepmother inspired my father to enter Louisville Dental College and become a dentist, and paid for his training with the life insurance money she received from the death of her first husband.

With the income from that investment in my father, she sent her three children and my younger brother through college and started each of them on the road to mastery of poverty.

As for myself, she was instrumental in placing me in a position where the late Andrew Carnegie gave me an opportunity such as no other author ever received—an opportunity which permitted me to learn from more than five hundred of the top-ranking, successful men who collaborated with me in giving the world a practical philosophy of personal achievement. A philosophy based on the "know-how" of my collaborators, gained from their lifetime experiences.

Source: *You Can Work Your Own Miracles.* Random House. 1996. Pgs. 75-76.

CHAPTER 3

*Learning is a treasure that will
follow its owner everywhere.*
—CHINESE PROVERB

Choosing a definite major purpose in our lives is truly a worthy choice. When we create a plan, and work the plan with faith and hope in a positive outcome, we intentionally forecast our life's end result, its fulfillment. From an acorn to an oak tree, from a caterpillar to a butterfly, from a seed to a blossom, we hold high expectations for potential outcomes for ourselves and others. By considering our early strengths and abilities we may begin to discern the plan for our lives that is being played out from birth. It seems easy enough, but is it?

Well meaning people often typecast their children into roles that they are not made for in life. They "see" a physician when the child wants to be a librarian. The "hold on" to athletic tendencies that appear in high school and label the teenager the next and upcoming great in some sport that the teenager has no interest in pursuing into the next stage of life. They "guide" a child toward the career they themselves could not achieve due to life's challenges and setbacks.

However, when we consider the fate of the acorn, the caterpillar, and the seeds of various sorts, whatever is unique within each of them plays out to the fulfillment of their abilities. This is the innate blessing from birth. As difficult as it may be to accept, each of us is headed to our special destination from birth, and the journey that gives us peace, contentment, and fulfillment, is the one that matches our blueprint, our genetic code, our uniqueness that is provided at birth by the Creator,

Infinite Intelligence, and is the treasure within ourselves.

This week's children's story is the adaptation of an American Folktale, *The Tale of Three Trees*. It is retold by Angela Elwell Hunt and is illustrated by Tim Jonke. It begins with "*Once upon a mountaintop, three little trees stood and dreamed of what they wanted to become when they grew up...*"

As the story unfolds, the wishes, or definite major purpose, of each little seedling is stated.

Little tree one states: *"I will be the most beautiful treasure chest in the world."*

Little tree two states: *"I will be the strongest ship in the world."*

Little tree three states: *"I will be the tallest tree in the world."*

Days, weeks, months, and years pass, and the trees are felled for the three woodcutters' uses. The story then reveals what happens to each of them. The little trees' statements of their purpose is fulfilled, but in ways they could not even imagine.

It seems to me that our lives take twists and turns on the rocky roads of life to bring us to our destiny also. Infinite Intelligence hands us the ingredients for our success at birth. Our choices carry us to our fulfillment in due time. Napoleon Hill reminds us to be faithful rather than fearful. Faith and fear cannot co-exist. To be faithful means to believe in the goodness of the Universe and that nothing can interfere with the Creator's plan for us. Faithfulness eases our trek in life while fearfulness constantly throws up roadblocks and dead ends. Anxiety and nervousness accompany fear, and peace, contentment, and acceptance accompany faith.

Consider the tale of the three trees, and cultivate the true abilities of children who are your own or who you influence. Learn to allow their abilities to grow and compliment them on their movement toward becoming that very precious something unique that they were put here to become at birth.

Your Mind is Your Master
by Napoleon Hill

You had nothing to do with your coming into this world. You may have little or nothing to do with your leaving it. But you have almost everything to do with your life while you possess that life. You can be the master of your fate, the captain of your soul by the simple process of taking possession of your own mind and using it to guide your own life without meddling in the lives of others.

Notice the connection between mastering yourself and not attempting to master others. A major reason for unhappiness is the tendency to meddle with the lives of others while we take too little time in trying to perfect our own.

Nobody else can do the job of taking possession of your mind, nor should you permit anyone else to try. Your mind is your master; yet your mind can be such a kindly master that it responds to your needs and desires and finds ways to make them come true when they are definite. All other creatures on earth are bound throughout their lives by a fixed pattern of instinct from which they cannot escape. YOU are bound only by the pattern you set up in your own mind. YOU are limited by nothing else.

Source: *Grow Rich with Peace of Mind.* Random House. 1996. Pg. 128.

PRINCIPLE 2

The Mastermind Alliance

The Mastermind Alliance principle consists of an alliance of two or more minds working together in perfect harmony for the attainment of a definite objective. Success does not come without the cooperation of others. The Mastermind Alliance principle is a practical medium through which you may appropriate and use the full benefits of the experience, training, education, specialized knowledge, and native intelligence of others as completely as if it were your own. An active alliance of two or more minds, in a spirit of perfect harmony for the attainment of a common objective, stimulates each mind to a higher degree of courage than that ordinarily experienced, and paves the way for the state of mind known as Faith.

CHAPTER 4

*Coming together, sharing together,
working together, succeeding together.*
—ANONYMOUS

The Mastermind concept is a unique principle in Dr. Hill's philosophy of success. It requires individuals to work together for a common mission much as with teamwork, but with the addition of a "presence" that Hill refers to as "the Mastermind." Hill's belief is that when two or more minds come together in perfect harmony for a common purpose or mission, a third mind grows out of the blending of the other minds. This idea may be beyond a youngster's capacity to comprehend, however, if children are reminded of the effects working together can produce on outcomes, maybe they can begin to catch the idea of a mission having a life of its own. When the good of the whole is more than simply the sum of the individual parts, institutions such as schools, churches, not-for-profit organizations, and others produce outcomes that go beyond the usual expectations.

The story **Stone Soup** by Jon J. Muth is an adaptation of an old tale that captivates young listeners. This retelling of the tale involves three monks, Hok, Lok, and Siew, as they journey along seeking the nature of happiness. During their journey they encounter  villagers who are distrustful of them and are afraid to welcome them into their homes and community. Doors are locked and shutters latched as the monks enter the village. But, the wise monks are clever and work together to entice the villagers to make soup from stones. Their interest captured, the villagers—one by one—come outside of their homes. Soon they realize that with their simple contribution of carrots, onions, potatoes, a piece of meat, or simply salt, that they have much to contribute. And, the amazing part is that when they do join in, much more comes back to them in return. The law of compensation and the law of increasing returns are both set into motion just because someone decided to take initiative and act.

This story can be introduced to children as a way in which their special gifts can be contributed to the outside world. By asking them what they have to offer, they can begin to think of their specialized talents and possessions as something that needs to be put out there in order to make the world a better place in which to live. A meal of only carrots or potatoes is not too appetizing, but when blended together a savory soup is cooked up for all to enjoy as a hearty meal. Children can begin to understand that their contribution is important even if it is only small, and by everyone adding something to the mix, great results can begin to take shape.

The contribution that children see themselves making at an early age creates in them a spirit of sharing and community that will serve them well as they grow into adulthood. By coming together for the common good and enjoying the outcome together, children can be taught to understand that working together has it merits. Pride can be attained too from working together and experiencing the fact that even a little can go a long way. Sharing and caring are traits that this story develops as well as the concept that there is an overview of all the good that can be produced when people work together for a common good.

Why not make some Stone Soup tonight by asking youngsters for help in the kitchen? By seeing what they can add to the pot, you will know where they are in becoming community minded members who can make a real difference in the world they are entering.

The Power of the Mastermind
by Napoleon Hill

It is quite probable that the mind is made up of a substance or energy, similar to the ether (if not, in fact, enough to form a contact, the mixing of the units of this "mind stuff" (let us call it the electrons of the ether) sets up a chemical reaction and starts vibrations which affect the two individuals pleasantly or unpleasantly.

The effect of the meeting of two minds is obvious to even the most casual observer. Every effect must have a cause. What could be more reasonable than to suspect that the cause of the change in mental attitude of the two minds, which have just come into contact, is in fact the disturbance of the electrons or units of each mind as they rearrange themselves in the new field created by the contact?

For the purpose of establishing this philosophy upon a sound foundation, we have gone a long way toward success by admitting that the meeting or coming in close contact of two minds sets up in each of those minds a certain noticeable "effect" or state of mind quite different from the one existing immediately prior to the contact. While it is desirable, it is not essential to know the "cause" of this reaction of mind upon mind. That the reaction takes place in every instance is a known fact, which gives us a starting point from which we may show what is meant by the term "mastermind."

A mastermind may be created through the bringing together or blending of two or more minds in a spirit of perfect harmony toward a specific objective. Out of this harmonious blending, the chemistry of the mind creates a third mind which may be appropriated and used by one or all of the individual minds. This mastermind will remain available as long as the friendly, harmonious alliance between the individual minds exists. It will disintegrate and all evidence of its existence disappear the moment the friendly alliance is broken.

Source: ***Succeed and Grow Rich Through Persuasion.*** The Napoleon Hill Foundation. Penguin Books. 1991. Pgs. 167-168.

CHAPTER 5

Two heads are better than one.
—PROVERB

A very favorite old English tale is ***The Little Red Hen.*** The tale is told in various ways, however, the message or theme remains the same. The little Red Hen works hard every day while others in the household rest and do nothing. One of her projects is planting and harvesting wheat to use for baking. The process from seed to flour is a long one, and she asks those in the household for help with the sowing, weeding, harvesting, grinding, and transporting. But, no one helps her. Eventually, she is ready to use the flour to bake bread. Soon, the wonderful aromas fill the house and all the others gather around the table ready to share in the result of the Little Red Hen's labor. The Little Red Hen refuses to share the bread. She eats it by herself thereby teaching the others a valuable lesson. And, the very next time she requested help, the others complied. They were then rewarded with the fruits of their labors as she bakes up a good reward for all to enjoy this time.

Some say this is selfish on the part of the Little Red Hen, but I disagree. She shows others both the value of being self-sufficient as well as the value of working together for shared outcomes. In order to encourage those who only want to capitalize on the work of others, she refuses to share the bread. But, she trades the teachable moment into a learning opportunity when she begins the process again and invites everyone to join in and contribute to the common good, or beneficial end results. The story comes full circle. It does not end with the Little Red Hen's refusal to share, but ends with the household members now understanding that the sharing of both the work and the reward is what the process is all about.

Engaging a Mastermind is a process. Each member must be invited to join and make an equal contribution. When the goal is achieved, each member shares evenly in the outcome. It is a process that works because the work is shared and the burden thereby is lighter for each member in the group. Children benefit from being taught this concept early on and learning that many hands make light work. Instilling this value in them from birth will make lessons regarding work and life more easily learned.

❖❖❖❖❖❖❖❖❖❖❖❖❖❖❖❖❖❖❖❖❖❖

The Mastermind Power Principle
by Napoleon Hill

Having clearly defined your goals and purposes in thought and in writing, it is advisable to select an individual or individuals with whom you can share your plan for achieve-ment. The mastermind principle is defined as an alliance of two or more people, working together in a spirit of perfect harmony to accomplish a definite purpose. The value of the "gathering together of those of like mind" is self-evident. Harmony in a home results when a man and woman work toward the establishment of a relationship that is mutually satisfying and productive of comfort and happiness for both.

Your mutual agreement with your employer to work toward high sales is a form of masterminding. If your major purpose in life is an ambitious one that extends beyond the accumulation of the ordinary requirements of subsistence, you will probably need the help of others in achieving it.

The mastermind principle is a means by which you may use the experience, the education, the talent, the influence, and perhaps the finances of other people to aid you in carrying out your major purpose. Your mastermind alliance may begin with your association with one other person. The number of alliances you will require directly depends entirely on the nature and the extent of the purposes of your alliance. A "meeting of the minds" must be regular, must be mutually beneficial, and must always be harmonious in the basic matters of sincerity and trust.

Source: *Succeed and Grow Rich Through Persuasion.* The Napoleon Hill Foundation. Penguin Books. 1991. Pgs. 79-80.

CHAPTER 6

*For the life of the wolf is the pack
And the life of the pack is the wolf.*
—UNKNOWN

Perhaps you have read Aesop's fable about the Lion and the Mouse. One day a mouse accidentally disturbs the King of the Jungle and begs not to be eaten. The Lion, feeling magnanimous, sets the mouse free while laughing about the Mouse's promise to save his life one day. Without further expectation, the Lion spares the Mouse and soon forgets the promise.  Months later, the Lion is hopelessly entangled in a hunter's trap. True to his word, the Mouse appears and works hard in gnawing the ropes holding the Lion. Once the Lion is freed, he acknowledges the Mouse as a true friend.

Although the story is simple, the message regarding the Mastermind Alliance is a great one. People of lower social status, reduced finances, different backgrounds, and certain qualities others may view as inferior to their own, can and do make surprising contributions. No one is meaningless. No one is without merit. No one deserves to be dishonored because they appear to be less than the norm. Whether you are the King of the Jungle or the Little Mouse is insignificant. The gifts you are given are those you are meant to share.

I like the saying, "I've got your back." When you hear this from a friend you know that you can proceed with confidence in whatever you are doing. If that first step is a fearful one, it helps if someone if behind you ready to catch you if you fall. Also, if there is someone who has your best interests at heart and then advises you as to what you may or may not consider doing, it can save you a great deal of turmoil later. Being part of the Master Mind groups that Dr. Hill discusses enable us to have a support staff of people at our beck and call. Likewise, they have us to count on when they have a need too. What better security is there in life than the knowledge and the experiences of those friends who can advise and assist you? Why not cultivate these alliances now and see how you can have a tremendous jumpstart and lift off in your life? It is a sure fire way to pave your road to success.

★★★★★★★★★★★★★★★★★★★★★★

Two Types of Master Mind
by Napoleon Hill

There are two general types of *master mind alliances*. One type is for purely social or personal reasons, consisting of one's relatives, friends and religious advisors, where no material gain is sought. The other type is the occupational, business or professional alliance consisting of individuals who have a motive of a material or financial nature—in other words, an economic alliance designed to help you sell your personal services, your skill, your ability, or to help you succeed in business.

Educational Activity. No man is ever through learning. If your major purpose in life is aimed above the average, you must continue to learn from every possible source, and especially where you can acquire knowledge particularly related to your purpose. Books in the public library make available to you the entire accumulated experience of mankind all highly organized and presented to you in concise forms. All they require of you in return is your effort in reading and studying them. Another source of knowledge and information too often overlooked is found in your daily life. By carefully choosing your friends and associates you can acquire a liberal education in a variety of subjects by the very enjoyable medium of conversation. This is a rich source of help, and one that you can tap by carefully selecting a social *master mind* group who will find the exchange mutually beneficial.

Religious Activity. We advocate no specific religion, but recognize the value of the contacts one may make in associating with church groups. These spiritual experiences enrich life, and the church or synagogue brings people together under favorable and harmonious circumstances. Often an alliance with members of your religious faith can be of immeasurable service to you in the furtherance of your definite major purpose.

Political Activity. Since the preservation of our privilege of becoming self-determining depends largely on keeping our government as it was intended to be, every citizen has a solemn responsibility to become informed on the political issues of the day and to vote intelligently. Political affiliation is also a source of contact which is often quite valuable.

Social Activity. This is a way to become acquainted with people with whom you can enjoy an exchange of helpful ideas. Here is where your wife or husband can be of tremendous assistance to you. A mind—to remain brilliant, alert, receptive and flexible—must constantly have the companionship of other minds. The medium of the *master mind* fulfills this requirement as nothing else can.

An Economic Alliance. No man can achieve greatness alone. Every outstanding success is based on cooperative effort. For instance, take the modern transportation and communication systems which cover our nation. They offer services which have never been achieved elsewhere. Using the *principle of the master mind,* they have combined all the resources necessary to implement and maintain elaborate organizations, coordinating the efforts of thousands of men and women for a single purpose.

Source: **PMA Science of Success.** Educational Edition. The Napoleon Hill Foundation. 1983. Pgs. 73-74.

PRINCIPLE 3

Applied Faith

Faith is an active state of mind. This belief in yourself is applied to achieving a definite major purpose in life. Faith is an abstract idea, a purely mental concept. Faith is the activity of individual minds facing themselves and establishing a working association with Infinite Intelligence. When a plan comes through to your conscious mind while you are open to the guidance of Infinite Intelligence, accept it with appreciation and gratitude and act on it at once. Do not hesitate, do not argue, challenge, worry, fret about it, or wonder if it's right. Act on it! Action is the first requirement of all faith. As the Bible states: "Faith without works is dead."

CHAPTER 7

The sun, the moon, the stars, the seas, the hills and the plains,
Are not these, O Soul, the Vision of Him who reigns?
                                                —LORD TENNYSON

The principle of Applied Faith is an active not passive system of belief. The key to living by faith, walking the talk, faking it before you make it, and remaining open to the infusion of Infinite Intelligence in our lives is believing in something beyond ourselves and then putting that belief into action. Without opening up to the wisdom of the Universe, we remain a closed container unable to fill the void inside. In order to complete the circuit we must be a doer instead of a receiver. The "Gimmie, Gimmie, Gimmie" attitude of "I believe so I can receive" must be replaced by the "Give, Give, Give" attitude of "I give so I can give back." Simply put, it is in giving that we receive, but the emphasis is on the doing not the taking.

This week's story is a parable for all ages about faith and encouragement. It is a metaphorical tale written by Jan Karon with illustrations by Robert Gantt Steele. Its title is ***The Trellis and the Seed.*** Everyday miracles occur when faith is applied and the gentle process of Mother Nature is allowed to follow its divine course.

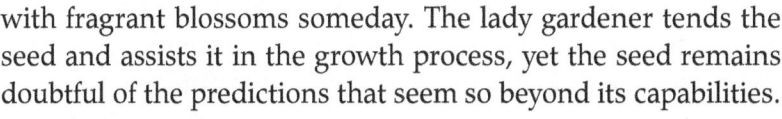

Basically, the story is about a tiny seed that is told it will become a beautiful vine with fragrant blossoms someday. The lady gardener tends the seed and assists it in the growth process, yet the seed remains doubtful of the predictions that seem so beyond its capabilities.

Through applied faith, the Nice Lady holds the promise of growth and beauty before the seed and takes action to assist the seed in the development process. As the seed sprouts, grows, and finally blossoms, the Nice Lady's prediction is fulfilled in due time. Admiring the vine's beauty she exclaims, "I just knew you were going to be something wonderfully different." Standing tall and beautiful on the trellis, the once tiny seed displays its exquisite beauty for her to enjoy.

Through Applied Faith both the Nice Lady and the Seed benefit from the interaction with Infinite Intelligence that produces the miraculous outcome. So too in our lives, when we have faith and hold that faith accountable by our doing, the Universe complies with the very end result that we envisioned all along. Right now it may be beyond our capacity to see into the future, but with Applied Faith we know fully that we are moving in the direction we are meant to travel. Putting one step in front of the other in an action oriented fashion guarantees our success if we plan our work and work our plan. Soon, if we practice Applied Faith, Infinite Intelligence will supply the results right on divine schedule. You just have to believe!

◆◆◆◆◆◆◆◆◆◆◆◆◆◆◆◆◆◆◆◆◆

An Explanation of Infinite Intelligence
by Napoleon Hill

At this point we would like to explain just what is meant by the term *Infinite Intelligence,* because it is our opinion that no one may ever reach the state of mind called *faith* without a positive, definite belief in a *Supreme Being.*

In arriving at such a belief and conviction, you may employ every faculty you possess. Observation, experimentation, feeling, prayer, meditation and thought are all legitimate approaches. As in all other activities you use your natural gifts, the sense of body and spirit, and the power of mind, to organize information and knowledge, so in this case, all methods by which facts are discovered may be used in establishing your contact with this *Supreme Power.*

*A man's religion should be worn in his heart –
not on the lapel of his coat.*

Man learns things primarily by seeing their effects or by accepting the statements of others whom he trusts. In the search for this basic reality, the *Infinite Power* behind all creation, you may look for evidence in the external universe, that which lies beyond the borders of your own body; you may look to your own inner self, by exploring as best you can the workings of your own mind; and you may examine the accumulated history of the race.

The external universe, to thinking men, has always been an evidence of the existence of a *Supreme, Creative, Directing Power.* The heavens today still remain the sublime object of our investigation and speculation; they are indeed witnesses of some great power at work. The advance of science reveals many secrets of the working of this power which we call nature. Every process of nature is orderly. No chance, disorder, or chaos has been seen in the physical universe. The sun does not rise in the East today and in the West tomorrow. All of the phenomena of nature are products of law; not a single exception has thus far been found. The universe exists under a reign of perfect law. Prevalent order, such obedience to law, clearly implied intelligent planning and *definiteness of purpose.* Order is the product of intelligent direction. Men of science today declare that the universe appears as a product of *thought!* That conclusion is inescapable. There can be not thought without a thinker. The universe declares that there is intelligent purpose in nature and that, therefore, there must be a supreme *Infinite Intelligence* directing it.

Source: **PMA *Science of Success.*** Educational Edition. The Napoleon Hill Foundation. 1983, Pgs. 83-84.

CHAPTER 8

The only limit to our realization of tomorrow will be our doubts of today. Let us move forward with strong and active faith.
—FRANKLIN DELANO ROOSEVELT

Last week I made my daughter-in-law Lupita cry. I knew I would, but I proceeded with my plan anyway. As you well know, these articles are dedicated to aligning children's stories with the 17 success principles of Napoleon Hill. The purpose of this year long activity is to reach out to parents, grandparents, and caregivers of young children so that they can begin to prepare the way for youngsters to understand the pathway to enduring success early in life. This week's focus is applied faith.

I have two grandchildren. Patrick who is four and Robbie who is two. Patrick is overcoming some learning disabilities and has delayed development now in the areas of language and speech. He has been introduced to English as his first language, but also Spanish and sign language. As with walking, he took he first steps later than normal, but immediately afterwards broke into running and even climbing ladders after his father who was working in the attic. So, he is definitely a late bloomer who is off to a great start.

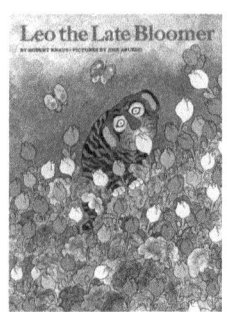

The story of applied faith that I shared with Lupita was **Leo the Late Bloomer.** It is a classic children's story about Leo who is delayed in his development. Pushed to bloom, Leo takes his own time to blossom and even with his father pushing full speed ahead, Leo lags behind. Only Leo's mother reminds everyone that Leo is just a late bloomer whose day to bloom will come in due time.

Leo the Late Bloomer is written by Robert Kraus with illustrations by José Aruego. The back cover reads:

Leo couldn't read. He couldn't write. He couldn't draw. He ate sloppily.

"What's the matter with Leo?" asked his father.

"Nothing," said his mother. "Leo's just a late bloomer."

Leo's mother was right. The one day, in his own good time, Leo bloomed!

I knew that this short children's classic touches hearts, minds and spirits. That is why Lupita cried. Dr. Hill tells us when emotions are joined with thoughts, the road to success is easier. By recognizing that everyone is unique and different, we each bloom right on our own schedule when we are ready to blossom, and not a moment before. As a mother, Lupita already knew this, but **Leo the Late Bloomer** just captured her emotions and reminded her that she has been doing the right thing all along. Remember–Thoughts + Emotionalized Actions = SUCCESS.

♦♦♦♦♦♦♦♦♦♦♦♦♦♦♦♦♦♦♦♦♦♦♦

The Hope for Future Achievement and the Capacity for Faith
by Napoleon Hill

Hope is the forerunner of the greatest of all states of mind, Faith! Hope sustains one in times of emergency when, without it, fear would take over. Hope is the basis of the most profound form of happiness which comes from the expectancy of success in some, as yet unattained, plan or purpose. Poor indeed is the person who cannot look toward the future with the hope that he will become the person he would like to be, or attain the position he would like to hold in life, or attain the objective he has failed to acquire in the past. Hope keeps the soul of man alert and active in his behalf, and *clears the line of communication by which Faith connects one with Infinite Intelligence.* Hope is a right royal person and the Divine Decorator of the other eleven riches of life.

Faith is the means of communication between the conscious mind of man and the great universal reservoir of Infinite Intelligence. It is the fertile soil of the garden of the human mind, wherein may be produced all the riches of life. It is the "eternal elixir" which gives creative power and action to the impulses of thought. It is the *élan vital* of the soul and it is without limitations. Faith is the spiritual quality which, when mixed with prayer, gives one direct and immediate connection with Infinite Intelligence. Faith is the power which transmutes the ordinary energies of thought into their spiritual equivalent, and it is the only means by which Infinite Intelligence may be appropriated to the uses of man.

Source: *You Can Work Your Own Miracles.* Random House. 1996. Pg. 81.

CHAPTER 9

Faith is the function of the heart.
—MAHATMA GANDHI

A children's story about belief, applied faith, and visualization that has endured the test of time is Margery Williams' classic tale *The Velveteen Rabbit,* subtitled *Or How Toys Become Real.* As you read the story and see in your mind's eye the detailed description of the little toy rabbit with its pink nose, button eyes, and string whiskers, you can conjure up an image from childhood that recalls such toys in the nursery. Perhaps you even had a similar toy that you played with, talked to, and took on outings in the backyard. As you think back and remember, these toys were not just playthings, rather, they had a life of their own and really were your imaginary playmates.

How different it is when we grow up! But, on second thought, is it really? We still imagine, daydream, and visualize our desires and many of those imaginings become real. Last year I shared with you my desire for a special puppy that I first saw in Alaska on a trip several years ago. I remembered that dog, called a Leonberger, and decided that when the time was right I would have one. The puppy only lived in my imagination for a long time, and I tried to locate a breeder with no success. I even contacted my niece Tricia who lived in Alaska at the time, and she said, "Auntie, there aren't any here."

Well, if you know anything about synchronicity, this is what happened. I was traveling to Houston with my husband and friend

Alan when we stopped to spend the night half way at a hotel. My husband is a patient at MD Anderson, so Alan was taking over some of the driving duties. Up early, I needed my coffee. Bob and I got into the elevator and as the door opened I was astonished to see an eight week old Leonberger puppy on a leash with his owner. I looked and recognized the breed. Impulsively, I asked the owner where he got him. He responded, "We just picked him up from a breeder in Indiana, and his name is Leo!" Amazing, a Leonberger in my own backyard. Leo's owner left the name of the breeder for me at the front desk, and I contacted her. Last weekend we drove to her home and put a deposit down on Olivia.

To me, I knew the puppy was real and I thought it into existence one desire at a time! Just like the Velveteen Rabbit, I envisioned what I wanted, knew it was out there because I saw "real" ones, and made it show up right on schedule. Whether this is truth in advance, conceive it, believe it, achieve it, applied faith, or the Universe delivering right on schedule, I will leave for you to decide. But, when that puppy stood outside the elevator looking at me, I knew that I would not have much longer to wait. My dream of a real Leonberger was standing there in reality looking back at me. How's that for synchronicity? You'll see it when you believe it—that is for certain.

So, read **The Velveteen Rabbit** to someone special and then ask them what they want to love into existence. You both will be the wiser for it!

✦✦✦✦✦✦✦✦✦✦✦✦✦✦✦✦✦✦✦✦✦

Free Yourself from Self-Imposed Limitations
by Napoleon Hill

The mind has been provided with a gateway of approach to *Infinite Intelligence* through what is known as the subconscious mind. From the vast reservoir of *Infinite Intelligence,* through the gateway of the *subconscious mind,* there flows into the conscious mind of man a continual stream of intelligence upon which we are dependent for our growth and development, and the unfolding of our innate powers. It is in this inflowing stream of intelligence that "we live and move and have our being."

Therefore, keep this gateway open. Keep it free from self-imposed limitations and restrictions. Do nothing which might stop this inflowing energy. *Infinite Intelligence* recognizes no limitations except those which we impose upon ourselves.

Whatever the mind of man conceives, man can achieve, so long as his conception does not run counter to any natural laws and is in harmony with a moral and orderly universe.

One of the purposes of man's existence here on earth seems to be to act as the receiver and distributor of the power of *Infinite Intelligence*. We can see that, to the extent that man cooperates in this purpose, he allies himself with the forces behind all nature. And, conversely, to the extent that he looks out only for his own selfish ends, he is opposing this power, or retarding its flow.

The power of *Infinite Intelligence* pours life into us as a flowing stream, maintaining all of the functions of our bodies and minds. We can use it to guide and govern the circumstances and conditions of our lives, if we will act as conductors of this energy, and shape it according to our constructive purposes.

This inflowing power has no limitations. It is forced to manifest itself in this world in a way in which we, as individuals, can understand and express it.

Life energy flows into a positive, receptive mind in a continual stream, just as strips of aluminum alloy are fed into the punch presses of a fabricating plant. Going into it is potential life, potential abundance, potential power, potential riches. But, like the forced aluminum strips, our thought *coming out* can be only what we have expressed—what the stamping machines of our own convictions and beliefs have impressed upon the original material.

Whatever we accept, whatever we love, cherish or desire with a burning desire and hold constantly in our thoughts as our own, finds fulfillment in our lives. As sunlight, passing through a prism, is broken up into its component color rays, so *Infinite Intelligence,* in passing through our conscious minds, takes on a variety of forms. The prism of our minds can be darkened only by the imperfections of our own creations of worry, fear and failure consciousness, which shut out all the lighter, happier colors. It is a stream of intelligence that starts through us, but just as a poorly made die in the punch press can cut rude and ugly pieces from the best of raw material, just as a faulty prism can turn beams of sunshine into shadows, so can our disbeliefs and doubts turn perfect life-energy into sickness, poverty, discord and misery.

The first essential then, is to be careful of the pattern of the die, to watch your desires and beliefs as carefully as the director of the United States Mint watches the die that casts the silver coins. Instead of picturing the things you fear and do not want, and thus stamping a negative on the *Infinite Intelligence* flowing into your mind, be sure to picture the conditions you do want.

If you would have faith, keep your mind on that which you want and off that which you do not want.

Source: **PMA *Science of Success Course*.** Educational Edition. The Napoleon Hill Foundation. 1983. Pgs. 87-89.

PRINCIPLE 4

Going the Extra Mile

Going the Extra Mile is the action of rendering more and better service than that for which you are presently paid. When you Go The Extra Mile, the Law of Compensation comes into play. This Universal Law neither permits any living thing to get something for nothing nor allows any form of labor to go unrewarded. You will find that Mother Nature goes the extra mile in everything that she does. She doesn't create just barely enough of each gene or species to get by; she produces an over abundance to take care of all emergencies that arise and still have enough left to guarantee the perpetuation of each form of life.

CHAPTER 10

*There is no exercise better for the heart
than reaching down and lifting people up.*
—JOHN ANDREW HOLMES

In discussing the principle of Going the Extra Mile, Napoleon Hill states:

> "The law of reaping increased returns by rendering more and better service than that for which you are paid is one of the basic laws of nature and has been recognized by scientists and philosophers for centuries."

This promise of accruing compound interest on compound interest from your investment is a pleasing one to consider. Every one of us likes to be paid what we are worth, but even more inviting is the concept of earning even more than we are worth just by activating the law of increased returns. This law is activated by doing more than you are paid to do without the expectation of an immediate return or even any return. The Universe keeps track of your "deposits" and all you have to do is keep on delivering above and beyond the usual expectation of service. Sooner or later, the account will shift in your favor and you will be the beneficiary of accrued interest from your investment of time and talent.

This is probably one of the easiest principles to practice since it requires little thinking and planning, but rather general giving. You do not have to even consider what it is that you will give. Instead, you just train yourself to see a need or an opportunity and then seize the moment. For example, does someone need help with opening a door, carrying groceries, handling luggage, picking up a dropped item, securing a recommendation, caring for a pet, servicing the car, receiving a ride to church or services, getting a note or card in the mail, helping with the laundry, receiving a word of praise, recognizing an achievement, or celebrating a special event? See how easy it is to generate a list? These are basic needs experienced by everyone one time or another. It is good to acknowledge them, but the service must be performed in order to receive the interest. It is not only the thinking, but the doing that activates the law.

The Dandelion Seed by Joseph Anthony and illustrated by Cris Arbo is a story that can help teach this concept to children of all ages. This little single seed remains attached to the dried dandelion flower, afraid to let go. But, eventually the seed is carried away on the wind and journeys far and wide. The mystery of where it will end up is unknown, but over time it lands in a nurturing spot, begins to grow, and  flowers into the dandelion it was meant to be. Its many leaves are shared by deer and rabbits, and bees and butterflies gather its nectar. Its purpose is in serving many, and soon it ripens into hundreds of seeds that are scattered everywhere. Finally, only one seed remains attached to the dandelion. The tiny seed is told to let go and see how the wind, rain, and sun will take care of it. Likewise, we are cared for by Infinite Intelligence and it is in the letting go that we truly become free and fulfill the purpose for which we were intended. By giving more than we get, our needs our met fully and ours seeds, or legacy, grows.

I invite you to consider the generosity of people who leave a legacy during their lifetime such as Andrew Carnegie, W. Clement Stone, and Napoleon Hill. Not only are they remembered for their generosity, but also for planting the seeds of education in libraries, books and the workplace that cause them to be remembered and highly regarded by generations yet unborn.

Going the Extra Mile
by Napoleon Hill

Render more and better service than that for which you are paid, and sooner or later you will receive compound interest on compound interest from your investment. For it is inevitable that every seed of useful service you sow will multiply itself and come back to you in overwhelming abundance.

If you will do this, you will be rewarded in several definite ways. You will sooner or later receive compensation far exceeding the actual value of the service you render. You will exhibit greater strength of character. You will find it easier to maintain a positive mental attitude at all times. You will find that there is a permanent market for your services. And you will experience the thrill of new and stronger convictions of courage and self-reliance, new surges of the self-starting power of personal initiative and an energizing influx of vital enthusiasm.

Source: **PMA Science of Success Course.** Educational Edition. The Napoleon Hill Foundation. 1983. Pg. 121.

CHAPTER 11

We are told to let our light shine, and if it does, we won't need to tell anybody it does. Lighthouses don't fire cannons to call attention to their shining—they just shine.
—DWIGHT L. MOODY

The Giving Tree by Shel Silverstein is a wonderful story for both the young and old. Told simply, the apple tree gives and gives unconditionally to a little boy who grows into a teenager, young man, adult, middle aged man, and finally an old man. Throughout the boy's life, the tree plays a stable part in the boy's journey of discovery and growth, both physically and spiritually.
It becomes his anchor for things currently happening and yet to come.

Perhaps there is a "tree" in your life that you return to time and again for reassurance, guidance, sustenance, and rest. Ask yourself what that might be in your life. How does it "go the extra mile" for you? What are its special gifts? Did you ever feel that this gift giving was a reciprocal process, or totally one-sided? Do you appreciate your touchstone, or just use it for your own personal needs? Why? After reading *The Giving Tree* what will you do differently? How will you acknowledge the goodness extended toward you? Why is it important to stop, consider, and next carry the benefit forward? Knowing what you have learned, how will you do that now?

The Giving Tree is a modern day parable about giving and receiving and someone's capacity for unconditional love. The little boy and the apple tree can both represent us at different stages in our lives. Are you a "giver" or a "taker?" Does giving come easily for you, or are you used to receiving? If you lack in one or the other, why not reverse your usual role and try on a new costume? Life truly is circular in motion, and when we experience both aspects of a concept we move toward wholeness. Next, if you are fond of parables, check out the Biblical ones and see if there are any lessons you may have overlooked or will benefit in reviewing! A lesson learned is a lesson we can carry with us for life.

✦✦✦✦✦✦✦✦✦✦✦✦✦✦✦✦✦✦✦✦✦

Go the Extra Mile
by Napoleon Hill

I have often been asked to give a man *something* to do that helps him leave resentment behind him; especially where his job and his career are concerned. The best possible action is this: go the extra mile.

Give more service and better service than you are paid for. Find out more about your job and the job above it than you absolutely have to know. Work in a way that makes your job do more than it is expected to do for the organization that employs you.

A young man was an estimator for a large printing firm. He didn't pay much attention to type faces, being content to let the customers go on using the type faces to which they were accustomed. This made his job easier—but, as I pointed out to him, it did nothing to qualify him as a man who really knows his job.

He studied type faces, arrangements of type on a page and other matters which lend effect and ever artistry to broadsides and brochures. When his boss received compliments on "the beautiful jobs you turn out," the boss realized what this young man was doing for his firm's reputation. The young man is now an executive of the firm, where before he was scarcely noticed. The young man also has relieved himself of a feeling of bitterness which might, in the end, have resulted in making him an old man with a mean little salary and a mean little soul.

Of course you don't have to feel mean and small and imposed upon before you go the extra mile!

A tonic in itself, the willingness to do more than you absolutely must is the hallmark of the big earner, the great leader, the happy and hearty person who day by day builds value into his life.

Source: *Grow Rich With Peace of Mind.* Random House. 1996. Pgs. 31-32.

CHAPTER 12

*Striving for success without hard work is like
trying to harvest where you haven't planted.*
—DAVID BLY

Don't you just love it when the main character in a story wins after working hard and long at a project? I do too. The payoff is well worth the added extra effort. As readers, we can see the specific end result that we are cheering for and hope that by the end of the story the character will earn his just rewards. Too bad life does not always follow suit! But that does not mean we give up. It means that we double up on our efforts, learn from our past mistakes, and pursue our goal with determination and renewed enthusiasm. As we throw our entire self into our mission, the Universe takes notice and brings us the outcome that we are so determined to achieve.

A very simple children's story teaches this lesson in a few pages. Written by Ruth Krauss, **The Carrot Seed** is about a little boy who won't give up. He goes about planting his carrot seed even though his family tells him that it won't come up! Undaunted by the naysayers, the little boy continues to weed and water the seed daily even though nothing seems to be happening. Father, mother, and big brother remind him that  "It won't come up." But, after not quitting and much persistence and going the extra mile daily, the carrot pops up! Just as the little boy knew all along it would.

Think back and remember when you were told something

wouldn't happen. Did you listen and stop trying or did you believe in your dreams and persist? The difference in what you did created the outcome you received. Think about it. Mother Nature always performs right on schedule, and if the Laws of the Universe are respected everything must work in tandem with each and every law. Never do Universal Laws work one day and not the next. They always and forever work because that is the Divine system we operate under. So, you see, the little boy with the single carrot seed understood the natural law of planting and reaping, and the carrot appeared just as he always knew it would.

What do you wish for? What do you work for? What do you intend to receive? The harvest is up to you. Get busy this season and begin planting that garden you visualize in your mind. The harvest always comes right on schedule! Just remember, "if it is to be it is up to me."

The Habit of Doing More Than You Are Paid For
by Napoleon Hill

People sometimes outgrow both their positions and their employers. More often, however, the reverse proves true.

Before deciding to change employers, take inventory of your employer and his business. Ascertain whether or not they offer you a future commensurate with your ability. If the analysis shows that an adequate opportunity exists where you are, develop that opportunity. You already have your foot inside the door. You have your employer's confidence or you would not be where you are. Capitalize this opportunity by making yourself indispensable and very soon the law of increasing returns will begin to reward you.

Every competent farmer understands and makes use of the law of increasing returns. He puts this law into operation in the following manner:

FIRST: He selects soil which is appropriate for the crop which he expects it to yield.

SECOND: He then prepares this soil by plowing and harrowing and perhaps by fertilization, so it will be favorable to the seed he plants.

THIRD: He plants seed which has been carefully selected for soundness, knowing that poor seed cannot yield a bountiful crop.

FOURTH: He then gives Nature a chance to compensate him for his labor through an appropriate period of time. He does not sow the seed one day and expect to reap a harvest the next.

Having taken these four steps, all of which have been in advance of his reward, the farmer knows that he will profit by the law of increasing returns when harvest time arrives and that he will get back from his labor not merely the amount of seed he planted in the soil, but a greatly increased quantity.

Source: *How To Sell Your Way Through Life.* The Napoleon Hill Foundation. 2005. Pgs. 152-153.

PRINCIPLE 5

Pleasing Personality

Personality is the sum total of one's mental, spiritual, and physical traits and habits that distinguish one from all others. It is the factor that determines whether one is liked or disliked by others. Your personality is your greatest asset or liability. It embraces everything you control—mind, body and soul. Some characteristics of a pleasing personality include: positive mental attitude, flexibility, sincerity, prompt actions, courtesy, tactfulness, pleasing tone of voice, smile, and tolerance.

CHAPTER 13

*Those who bring sunshine to the lives
of others cannot keep it from themselves.*
—JAMES M. BARRY

When you meet someone with a pleasing personality, they stand out from the crowd. Perhaps they hold the door for you as you enter a room, smile for no reason, appear well groomed, and talk with you instead of at you. All of these characteristics and more comprise the 29 traits Napoleon Hill identifies as factors of a pleasing personality. The good news is that you do not have to be born with them. You can cultivate them as you decide to acquire the traits for yourself.

Dr. Hill indicates the following components of a pleasing personality: a positive mental attitude, flexibility of mind, sincerity of purpose, promptness of decision, common courtesy, tactfulness, pleasing tone of voice, facial expression and the habit of smiling, tolerance, frankness in manner and speech, a keen sense of humor, faith in Infinite Intelligence, a keen sense of justice, the appropriate use of words, effective speech, control of the emotions, alertness of interest, versatility, fondness for people, control of temper, hope and ambition, temperance, patience, humility of heart, appropriateness of dress, effective showmanship, clean sportsmanship, the ability to shake hands properly, and personal magnetism.

This is quite a list, but the acquisition of each personal trait increases your potential personal worth.

A children's story by Tom Robinson and illustrated by Peggy Bacon entitled ***Buttons*** was first published in 1938. It details the story of an alley cat who becomes a gentleman due to the intervention of a little girl who rescues him after a fight. Buttons transitions from being the King of the Alley to the Lord of the Manor because he cultivated the traits of genuine pure-bred behavior. Instead of scratching he started purring, his fur went from matted to soft and smooth, and he worked on forgetting his home on the street, and instead pursued the life of a gentlemen. He learned the traits of spoiled housecats and soon had that coveted title himself. And it was all because he developed a pleasing personality.

Transformation can take place in each of us. First, however, we must learn that there is a better way and discard gruff behavior for polished performance. When we do, we are on the way to developing a pleasing personality and creating a wonderful new home for ourselves too.

✦✦✦✦✦✦✦✦✦✦✦✦✦✦✦✦✦✦✦✦✦

Pleasing Personality
by Napoleon Hill

A *pleasing personality* is the aggregate of all the agreeable, gratifying and likeable qualities of any one individual. The person who continually practices the habit of *going the extra mile* and daily employs the Golden Rule will inevitably also acquire a *pleasing personality*. And a *pleasing personality* is an asset none of us can do without if we wish to attain success. Why is this?

Because it is through one's *pleasing personality* that he motivates others to help him achieve the goals he desires, and, as we discovered in the lesson on the *master mind,* no one can attain notable success without the help of others.

Put a little differently, from birth until death every person engages in some type of *selling* every day of his life. And *selling* in the sense used here means winning *acceptance, approval or adoption.*

The newborn baby is a salesman from the first moment that it begins to breathe. It requires and desires good, which it procures by the simple sales method of crying to attract sympathy.

Later, during the child's early activities, he sells himself into possession of that which will gratify his needs and wants by the control of his personal conduct. It is during this time that he can learn how valuable pleasing behavior and right conduct toward others can be to him, for he has nothing else to offer.

After the child reaches the age of maturity, he begins to sell himself into the possession of his wants by a combination of his personal conduct and the service he renders to others. *The most important factor at this point of his career is the mental attitude in which he renders service.*

Mental attitude continues to be an important factor during the remainder of his life.

Source: ***PMA Science of Success.*** Educational Edition. The Napoleon Hill Foundation. 1983. Pg. 163.

CHAPTER 14

Our belief at the beginning of a doubtful undertaking is the one thing that ensures the successful outcome of our venture.
—WILLIAM JAMES

Pleasing Personality is often showcased in a person's interest and ability to help others. We remember people more who are considerate and helpful while interacting with us and most people working in the area of service need to intentionally cultivate qualities that make them more people oriented.

Think of the times that someone behind a desk has greeted you with a pleasant smile, a handshake, a "how can I help you?" question, and perhaps an offer of a cup of coffee or soft drink. Almost instantly you align with that person because they are placing you, the customer, first. When common courtesy prevails it seems that the world does go better.

A children's book that has always displayed this type of pleasing personality in action is **The Jolly Postman** by Janet and Allan Ahlberg. It is pleasing to both read and explore because actual letters are inserted within pockets in the pages. Just by receiving special, personalized letters, the characters in the stories become real and we as the readers also become engaged in what the Postman delivers to someone's door. It is almost as if we are looking over someone's shoulder and reading, with approval, their personal mail. There are several editions of this special book, but the first one captivates yet today. Mother Goose land has never been so alive and well.

Way before email and Facebook, this children's edition enchanted millions of readers because the Postman was jolly, and always delivered personalized messages on his route the old-fashioned way.

Why not take a moment and write a handwritten note or letter right now and put it in today's mail? You will surely receive a pleasant response because rather than taking less time to connect with someone you are making a more specialized effort to show someone that you care for them in a more meaningful way. That special note or letter could stick around for years and remind the recipient that you thought of them in a special way, and you wanted them to know it by your written message. And, the Jolly Postman will be happy to deliver it for you for just the cost of a Forever Stamp. Get busy. Write that message. And smile afterwards because you have just made someone feel special.

✦✦✦✦✦✦✦✦✦✦✦✦✦✦✦✦✦✦✦✦✦✦

The Need for Change
by Napoleon Hill

The real test of a man's belief in a positive mental attitude and of his faith is in the challenge of change which he must meet every day of his life. One of the first requirements for enduring faith and success is a capacity to accept and profit by change.

It has been said that the only permanent thing known to man is change. In order to preserve the faith which will give you power for the attainment of success, you must make yourself flexible enough to adjust to all types of change. If you are flexible, you will ride with the tide of change instead of going down under it.

Consider the following suggestions and determine which, if utilized, would strengthen the power of faith you need each day.

Change from the habit of thinking about and fearing the things you do not desire, to the habit of believing you can and will make life pay off on your own terms.

Change from the habit of thinking and talking of the physical ailments you may have or fear you will acquire to the habit of speaking and thinking of the perfect health you desire, until you develop a "health consciousness." Remember that imaginary ailments can do you as much harm as if they were real, if you accept them and encourage them by fear.

Change from the habit of desiring more material things than you need and can use, to the habit of sharing your riches so that they will serve others and thereby multiply themselves in your behalf.

Change from the habit of self-satisfaction to the habit of positive discontentment sufficient to keep you searching for more knowledge and wisdom to make your life richer both spiritually and materially.

Change from the habit of intolerance to the habit of open-mindedness on all subjects, toward all people, remembering that a closed mind doesn't grow, but atrophies and becomes powerless.

Change from the habit of fault-finding to the habit of looking for the good in other people and letting them know that you have discovered it. It is true that people will see in you whatever you see in them, be it good or bad.

Change from the habit of self-pity to the habit of facing facts about yourself and the real causes of your fears and worries. Remember that the looking glass will be helpful in making this change.

Change from the habit of speaking disparagingly of others to the habit of praising them, for this is also a habit which will inspire reciprocation.

While you are considering these suggestions, be sure to recognize the difference between your needs and your right to receive. We need many things which we have not earned the right to receive. The one sure way to obtain the right to receive is by going the extra mile, putting others under obligation to you by rendering more service and better service than that for which you are paid.

Source: *Succeed and Grow Rich Through Persuasion.* Penguin. 1992. Pgs. 154-155.

CHAPTER 15

*Time and money spent in helping men to do
more for themselves is far better than mere giving.*
—HENRY FORD

As we progress in our study of the 17 Success Principles, it may seem that several of the principles are very similar. In fact pleasing personality, personal initiative, and positive mental attitude have much in common. When considered as a unit, the principles do overlap yet support each other. If you compare it to a sandwich, the assembly and ingredients can be different yet the proposed outcome is the same—a wholesome meal. It is a good idea to see and comprehend how the principles support, intermingle, and transform a student's personality from the inside out. Pay close attention to how this works and then you will be able to heighten your awareness and apply the principles for advancement in your profession and in your home life.

A clever book by Jackie French and illustrated by Bruce Whatley entitled **Pete the Sheep-Sheep** tells the story of a sheep named Pete who is in charge of rounding up the sheep for shearing. Usually this is done by a sheep dog, however, sheep shearer Shaun does not have a sheep  dog. Shaun has a sheep named Pete. Pete has many of the pleasing personality traits, and he treats the sheep with respect and decorum. The sheep are delighted with this new approach since they were tired of having commands barked at them. Now they are treated with politeness, courtesy, and loving kindness as they head off to be sheared. Although this unconventional approach was working, the other sheep shearers and dogs were not happy because things were not being done in the traditional manner. Both Pete and Shaun had to go.

Instead of belly aching, back stabbing, and generally displaying a negative attitude, Shaun and Pete left their positions and opened a very successful Sheep Salon in town. Soon the sheep dogs visited the Salon to get a trim and a new improved look. And, as you may guess, the sheep shearers were next to experience the salon. Soon, everyone was looking gorgeous because a new idea took hold. The shearers accepted new positions in the salon as well. But, due to the increase in consumer support, the salon had to be renamed. Shaun's Animal Salon is now open for expanded service!

Just imagine what the traits of a pleasing personality can do for you and your business. Why not try some and see how very far they take you?

◆◆◆◆◆◆◆◆◆◆◆◆◆◆◆◆◆◆◆◆◆◆

Benefits of a Pleasing Personality
by Napoleon Hill

Since no one ever voluntarily does anything without a motive, and no one desires to labor without the promise of reward, let us briefly review the benefits one may enjoy when he develops a pleasing personality:

a. A *pleasing personality* attracts the friendly cooperation of others, and thus prepares the way for *master mind alliances*.
b. It insures the maintenance of a *positive mental attitude* which is a prerequisite for success in all constructive human endeavor.
c. It qualifies one with the most important fundamental of leadership in any calling or profession.

d. It establishes harmony with one's own mind, which is the first requirement for harmony in relationships with others.
e. It is an essential asset for the accumulation of material riches.
f. It is a builder of self-reliance.
g. It helps convert defeat into victory.
h. It increases the space one may occupy in the hearts of others.
i. It discourages friction in all human relationships.

A *pleasing personality* also brings other advantages. We have listed only the more important ones, but any one of them alone is sufficient to justify all the effort put into the development of a *pleasing personality.*

There are those who believe that a *pleasing personality* is an inherent quality with which only a few are endowed at birth. Perish the thought! A *pleasing personality* is an asset of priceless value which can be attained by those who are willing to pay the price of its development. And an important part of this price is a sincere, wholesome love of people.

Source: **PMA *Science of Success Course*.** Educational Edition. The Napoleon Hill Foundation. 1983. Pgs. 195-196.

PRINCIPLE 6

Personal Initiative

"There are two types of men," said Andrew Carnegie, "who never amount to anything. One is the fellow who never does anything except that which he is told to do, the other is the fellow who never does more than he is told to do. The man who gets ahead does the thing that should be done without being told to do it, but he does not stop there, he goes the extra mile by doing a great deal more than is expected or demanded of him." Personal Initiative is the power that inspires the completion of that which one begins. It is the power that starts all action. No person is free until he learns to do his own thinking and gains the courage to act on his own Personal Initiative—it is the twin brother of Going the Extra Mile.

CHAPTER 16

The difference between getting somewhere and nowhere is the courage to make an early start.
—CHARLES M. SCHWAB

Personal Initiative is essential for the application of the achievement of one's definite major purpose in life. Simply having a definite major purpose without a clear cut plan of action for its attainment via the application of personal initiative would make having a definite major purpose absolutely worthless. It would be comparable to having the greatest intention in the world, but without action toward that intention, the intention becomes meaningless.

Napoleon Hill reminds us that the seventeen success principles of this philosophy are related to each other just like the links of a chain. No single principle can bring a person ultimate success. But a combination of them with corresponding application can bring about the desired form of success.

There is a legend told about St. Francis of Assisi and the Wolf of Gubbio. Francis dedicated his life's mission to his overpowering belief in the brotherhood of all living things. When an old wolf left his pack and plagued the citizens of neighboring Gubbio, they became frightened and stayed indoors. Children no longer played outdoors, the village market was  shut down, sheep and livestock were penned and not taken to graze on the hillside, and fear overtook the citizenry. A single villager, the baker, left Gubbio and traveled to Assisi asking

Francis to intervene. Francis agreed to mediate the situation with the wolf and headed back to the village with the baker.

Soon Francis was in front of the wolf's den and called him out. The wolf was old, frightened, and hungry. Francis told the wolf that there was enough for everyone and food can be shared. Francis received a pledge from the wolf that he would harm no one in the village and, in return, the townspeople promised to feed and care for the wolf.

And so, it came to pass that St. Francis' dedication to the brotherhood of all living things came to pass due to the Saint's personal initiative. The wolf became a member of every family in town and he was never hungry. For two years the people and the wolf lived out their agreement. Dying of old age, the wolf was mourned as if he were a member of the community. Truly, he had become one the very day he pledged to St. Francis that he would harm no one. That is why the story of **Brother Wolf of Gubbio** is told yet today.

✦✦✦✦✦✦✦✦✦✦✦✦✦✦✦✦✦✦✦✦✦

Move on Your Own Personal Initiative
by Napoleon Hill

The mind that has been made to receive, attracts that which it needs, just as a magnet attracts steel filings.

The most difficult part of any task is that of making a start. But once it has been made, the way to complete the job become evident. The truth of this has been proved by the fact that men with *definite major purposes* are more successful than those without objectives.

And we have yet to find a successful man who did not readily admit that the turning-point of major importance in his life came when he adopted a *definite major purpose.*

No one person can tell another what his *definite major purpose* in life should be. But any successful man will verify that success is not possible without such a purpose.

Adopt a *definite major purpose* and see how quickly the habit of moving on your own personal initiative will inspire you to action.

Your imagination will become more alert and it will reveal to you many opportunities related to your purpose. Opposition to your purpose will disappear and people will give you their friendly cooperation.

Fear and doubt will disappear also. And somewhere along the way you will meet your "other self" face to face—that self which can, and will, carry you over to the success side of the River of Life.

From there on the going will be easy and the way will be clear, for you will have adapted yourself to the great intangible forces of nature which lead inevitably to the attainment of your chosen goal.

You will wonder why you did not find the path sooner, and you will understand why success attracts more success while failure attracts more failure.

And just a short distance ahead, you will see the great gate that leads into Happy Valley! You are not there yet, for there are lesser gates through which you must pass before you enter the great estate.

Source: *PMA Science of Success Course.* Educational Edition. The Napoleon Hill Foundation. 1983. Pgs. 206-207.

CHAPTER 17

Never make a case against yourself.
—DR. NORMAN VINCENT PEALE

Personal Initiative is the principle of success that enables you to change "I can'ts" into "I cans." At times things may seem so difficult that you truly believe there is nothing that you can do right. Negativity sets in and positivity runs out the door. You see yourself at a standstill because the mountain in front of you won't reduce into the conquerable molehill, and all seems beyond your capability. Looking through dark colored glasses, this world view isn't a pretty one. "How does a person overcome this inability to perform?" you ask yourself. Well, the answer is right at your feet—get out of bed and get moving! Personal initiative requires taking more control over your physical self rather than your mental self. Actually, thinking too much can slow you down.

Once upright, the next question is what do I do now? The simple answer, anything. Just get moving. Our bodies are made for physical movement and when our mind is in synchronization with our bodies they work best in tandem. We all know the phrases—"Do It Now!," "Do First Things First," and "Eat the Frog First." Agreeably all these motivational mantras help to make the mind shift to the positive side, but they do not work unless the commands for action are followed. "Do" and "Eat" are action words that challenge us to move.

Jam & Jelly by Holly and Nellie is a children's book that focuses on taking personal initiative to acquire a much needed coat for the cold winter months in Northern Michigan. Written by Gloria Whelan, this story develops the idea of using personal initiative and what one already has to transform something available such as local berries into something needed—a warm winter coat for school. Using both personal initiative and creative vision, Holly's mother doesn't back down from the problem or lament her circumstances, instead she gets busy making jellies and jams with her daughter that will be sold to earn monies for the coat. Once the plan is in place, and mother and daughter work the plan, the good result is inevitable.

Life brings us many situations of "I can'ts." If we allow these threats to defeat us, they will. Always remember to list those things you can do to resolve a situation, rather than those things you cannot do. Therein lies the seed of an equal or greater benefit. The kernel of hope that oftentimes remains hidden in the adversity. There are things Holly can do and things her mother can do, and they are not the same. But combining these things together through the principle of personal initiative enables the outcome to be a positive one—a new, warm winter coat for school.

Try the secret ingredient of personal initiative today in your own life. The outcome will bring sweeter results rather than if you remained a sourpuss and only wallowed in your difficulties. Have high hopes and your intention will create your positive outcome.

♦♦♦♦♦♦♦♦♦♦♦♦♦♦♦♦♦♦♦♦♦

Symptoms of the Fear of Criticism
by Napoleon Hill

Criticism is the one form of service, of which everyone has too much. Everyone has a stock of it which is handed out, gratis, whether called for or not. One's nearest relatives often are the worst offenders. It should be recognized as a crime (in reality it is a crime of the worst nature), for any parent to build inferiority complexes in the mind of a child, through unnecessary criticism. Employers who understand human nature, get the best there is in men, not by criticism, but by constructive suggestion. Parents may accomplish the same results with their children. Criticism will plant FEAR in the human heart, or resentment, but it will not build love or affection.

Symptoms of the fear of criticism:

This fear is almost as universal as the fear of poverty, and its effects are just as fatal to personal achievement, mainly because this fear destroys initiative, and discourages the use of imagination.

The major symptoms of the fear are:

SELF-CONSCIOUSNESS. Generally expressed through nervousness, timidity in conversation and in meeting strangers, awkward movement of the hands and limbs, shifting of the eyes.

LACK OF POISE. Expressed through lack of voice control, nervousness in the presence of others, poor posture of body, poor memory.

PERSONALITY. Lacking in firmness of decision, personal charm, and ability to express opinions definitely. The habit of side-stepping issues instead of meeting them squarely. Agreeing with others without careful examination of their opinions.

INFERIORITY COMPLEX. The habit of expressing self-approval by word of mouth and by actions, as a means of covering up a feeling of inferiority. Using "big words" to impress others, (often without knowing the real meaning of the words).

Imitating others in dress, speech and manners. Boasting of imaginary achievements. This sometimes gives a surface appearance of a feeling of superiority.

EXTRAVAGANCE. The habit of trying to "keep up with the Joneses," spending beyond one's income.

LACK OF INITIATIVE. Failure to embrace opportunities for self-advancement, fear to express opinions, lack of confidence in one's own ideas, giving evasive answers to questions asked by superiors, hesitancy of manner and speech, deceit in both words and deeds.

LACK OF AMBITION. Mental and physical laziness, lack of self-assertion, slowness in reaching decisions, easily influenced by others, the habit of criticizing others behind their backs and flattering them to their faces, the habit of accepting defeat without protest, quitting an undertaking when opposed by others, suspicious of other people without cause, lacking in tactfulness of manner and speech, unwillingness to accept the blame for mistakes.

Source: *Think and Grow Rich.* A Ballantine Book, Published by Random House Publishing Group 1960. Pgs. 210-211.

CHAPTER 18

He that would have fruit must climb the tree.
—THOMAS FULLER

Personal Initiative unlocks the door to personal achievement. Without taking those precarious first steps under the influence of personal initiative no dream can be fulfilled. Procrastination is the reason so few people ever move forward in procuring their dreams. When we procrastinate we are telling ourselves that for whatever reason we do not have the energy, talent, motivation, inspiration, willpower, desire, aim, energy, enthusiasm, etc., to move toward our goal. In a lock down fashion, procrastination is the enemy that defeats us before we start. By jolting ourselves out of this process of stagnation, we open the doors to our life's work.

Angelina Ballerina by Katharine Holabird and illustrated by Helen Craig is a children's story filled with unbounded energy, enthusiasm, and action. The little mouse heroine only desires one thing in life, and that is to dance as a ballerina. Daily, she pretends, she makes believe, and she practices dance moves that an aspiring ballerina would make.  She focuses on being a ballerina at school, at home, and even in her dreams to the exclusion of everything else. She is becoming a nuisance and her parents express concern. Mother Mouse discusses the growing problem with Father Mouse. Mr. Mouse suggests a solution, and with gift box in hand, he and Mrs. Mouse present Angelina a pair of ballet slippers and a pink ballet dress. Next, they enroll her in Miss Lilly's Ballet School where she can dance and practice to her heart's content. Her definite chief aim of becoming a real ballerina is taking shape. Soon, Angelina begins to clean her room, to be on time for school, and to behave better at home. Her heart's desire is being met, and she no longer dreams about becoming a ballerina. Instead she is growing into one!

This touching story details the simple beginnings of a life's career. Fortunately, Angelina's parents recognize her interest and budding talent and help her begin to fulfill her life's mission. By paying attention to where our interests and energy take us, we too can learn where our hidden talents are waiting for fulfillment. The saying "leap and the net will appear," applies to each of us. We must risk looking childish, foolish, and unaccomplished, if someday we are to become a leader in our field.

✦✦✦✦✦✦✦✦✦✦✦✦✦✦✦✦✦✦✦✦✦✦

The Pass-Key that Opens the Door to Opportunity
by Napoleon Hill

A great philosopher once said: *"Initiative is the pass-key that opens the door to opportunity."*

I do not recall who this philosopher was, but I know that he was great because of the soundness of his statement.

We will now proceed to outline the exact procedure that you must follow if you are to become a person of *initiative and leadership*.

First: You must master the habit of *procrastination* and eliminate it from your make-up. This habit of putting off until tomorrow that which you should have done last week or last year or a score of years ago is gnawing at the very vitals of your being, and you can accomplish nothing until you throw it off.

The method through which you eliminate *procrastination* is

based upon a well known and scientifically tested principle of psychology which has been referred to in the two preceding lessons of this course as Autosuggestion.

Copy the following formula and place it conspicuously in your room where you will see it as you retire at night and as you arise in the morning:

Initiative and Leadership

Having chosen a *definite chief aim* as my life-work I now understand it to be my duty to transform this purpose into reality.

Therefore, I will form the habit of taking some definite action each day that will carry me one step nearer the attainment of my *definite chief aim.*

I know that *procrastination* is a deadly enemy of all who would become leaders in any undertaking, and I will eliminate this habit from my make-up by:

    a. Doing some one definite thing each day, that ought to be done, without anyone telling me to do it.

    b. Looking around until I find at least one thing that I can do each day, that I have not been in the habit of doing, and that will be of value to others, without expectation of pay.

    c. Telling at least one other person, each day, of the value of practicing this habit of doing something that ought to be done without being told to do it.

I can see that the muscles of the body become strong in proportion to the extent to which they are used, therefore I understand that the *habit of initiative* is in the small, commonplace things connected with my daily work, therefore I will go at my work each day as if I were doing it solely for the purpose of developing this necessary *habit of initiative.*

I understand that by practicing this habit of taking the initiative in connection with my daily work I will be not only developing that habit, but I will also be attracting the attention of those who will place greater value on my services as a result of this practice.

Signed _____

Regardless of what you are now doing, every day brings you face to face with a chance to render some service, outside of the course of your regular duties, that will be of value to others. In rendering this additional service, of your own accord, you of course understand that you are not doing so with the object of receiving monetary pay. You are rendering this service because it provides you with ways and means of exercising, developing and making stronger the aggressive spirit of *initiative* which you must possess before you can ever become an outstanding figure in the affairs of your chosen field of life-work.

Source: *Law of Success in Sixteen Lessons.* The Original Unedited Edition. Volume II. The Napoleon Hill Foundation. 2013. Pgs. 8-9.

PRINCIPLE 7

Positive Mental Attitude

Positive Mental Attitude is the right mental attitude in all circumstances. Keep your mind on the things you want and off the things you don't want. Remember the old French proverb: "Be very careful what you set your heart on, for you will surely achieve it." Success attracts more success while failure attracts more failure. This principle presents the means by which the entire philosophy can best be assimilated and put to practical use. You cannot get the most out of the other sixteen principles without understanding and applying this one.

CHAPTER 19

Great men are they who see that the spiritual is stronger than any material force, that thoughts rule the world.
—RALPH WALDO EMERSON

Remember the sentence—**A positive mental attitude is the right mental attitude in all circumstances.** Turn these words over in your mind and really consider what they mean. There is only one mental attitude to cultivate at all times and that is a positive one, never a negative one. Holding negative attitudes will never make you a positive person, so it is not worth the time you spend on them. Thinking about, dwelling upon, and acting upon all the negative emotions that humans engage—fear, hatred, anger, envy, greed, jealousy, revenge, irritability, and superstition—will never contribute to your desired success. Each of these negative emotions creates a downward spiral that makes the hole we dig for ourselves harder and harder to climb out of because we are moving in the wrong direction.

When moving in the wrong direction, just recall the special children's book that was read to many of us as youngsters—*The Little Engine That Could!* by Watty Piper. Instead of going downhill, this little engine wants to make it up a very big incline with all its heart and soul, but the hill  is steep, and energy is at a premium, and rather than backing down, the little engine just decides to repeat the self-suggestion "I think I can, I think I can, I think I can" as it struggles to make it to the top of the hill.

After much huffing and puffing and inward struggle, finally, almost miraculously, the little engine reaches the peak and glories in its accomplishment. How did it achieve this improbable outcome?—by thinking! Thinking with a Positive Mental Attitude and belief in the outcome causes the little engine to exert every ounce of energy it has, and it turns out to be enough.

We know that our belief in our ability to achieve the outcome we want determines our outcome. In this way we actually create our destiny, our future, with one "I think I can, I think I can" mantra at a time. It seems silly to say this, but whether you think you can, or you think you can't, you are correct. So, it is natural to assume that whether we choose to end up on the highest mountaintop or remain in the deepest valley of despair, it is our thinking that makes it so! Be Positive. Think only those thoughts that hold you to the goodness you deserve and that you want to call into your life. Always remember the Little Engine That Could and you will give yourself that additional push in life by saying over and over again, I think I can, I think I can, I think I can. And you will!

✦✦✦✦✦✦✦✦✦✦✦✦✦✦✦✦✦✦✦✦✦✦

Development of a Positive Mental Attitude
by Napoleon Hill

A subject of paramount importance in the development and maintenance of a *positive mental attitude is believing where belief is justified.* Let us review some of the circumstances which call for belief:

- Acquire an enduring belief in the existence of *Infinite Intelligence* from which your Creator makes it possible for you to receive the power necessary to help you take possession of your own mind, and direct it to whatever ends you may choose.

- Acquire an enduring belief in your ability to become free and self-determining as your greatest gift from your Creator. You should demonstrate this belief in actions fitting to its nature.
- Believe in that way of life and form of government which guarantees the freedom and precious privileges for which men in every century and all parts of the world have fought and died.
- Believe in those with whom you are associated in your occupation or calling in life, and recognize that if they are not worthy of your complete belief, you have the wrong associates.
- Believe in the power of the spoken word and see to it that you speak no word which does not harmonize in every respect with your *positive mental attitude.*

Source: *PMA Science of Success Course.* Educational Edition. The Napoleon Hill Foundation. 1983. Pg. 231.

CHAPTER 20

Man can only receive what he sees himself receiving.
—FLORENCE SCOVEL SHINN

Napoleon Hill discusses the four advantages of deciding upon a definite major purpose combined with a positive mental attitude. When you do so, Dr. Hill states that four advantages appear almost magically to aid you. A fairy tale by the Brothers Grimm entitled *The Frog Prince* illustrates this process perfectly.

In brief, this story relates the trials and tribulations of a Prince who was placed under a spell by a spiteful fairy. The spell could only be reversed under certain improbable conditions. Now living as a Frog, the Prince remains optimistic and retains many of his positive human characteristics. While watching a Princess play nearby with a golden ball, he sees her throw it too high and it bounces into a  pond. She begins to cry and states that she would give everything she has in the world to get her favorite plaything back. The Frog hears her weeping. He asks her why she is crying. She immediately tells him that her golden ball has fallen into the pond and she cannot retrieve it. Knowing the conditions of his curse, he immediately sees his advantage. He promises to retrieve the ball if she agrees to the three conditions. She must love him, allow him to eat from her golden plate, and sleep on her bed. Thinking she has the upper hand, she agrees. The Frog dives after the ball as promised.

—Advantage 1 appears here. The Frog has established his

definite major purpose combined with PMA. He conceives it, believes it, and achieves it. He knows what he has to do, he sees himself doing it, and brings the golden ball back to the Princess.—

Overjoyed with her ball, she picks it up and runs back to the castle leaving the Frog behind. Undaunted, the Frog applies Advantage 2.

—**Advantage 2** appears here. He climbs out of the pond, and heads in the direction of the castle. He puts his goal into action.—

Arriving at the castle, he knocks at the door, and calls for the Princess to uphold her part of the bargain. Hearing the promise that she made, the King reminds her that she needs to remain true to her word. The King states: "As you have given your word you must keep it; so go and let him in."

The Frog dines with the Princess, eats from her plate, and sleeps on her satin pillow. When morning comes he leaves, and the Princess believes that she is finally done with him. But, he returns the second night to sleep on the same satin pillow.

—**Advantage 3 and Advantage 4** appear here. The Frog is determined to have what he wants. He takes action and plans on his success.—

He arrives the third night and sleeps once again on the satin pillow. When the Princess awakes on the third morning the Frog is gone and a handsome prince is standing at the head of her bed. He tells her about the enchantment and now because the spell is broken he wants to take her home, marry her, and love her for life. The Princess, of course, says "Yes."

In a nutshell, the Frog succeeds because he recognizes his opportunity since he knows the conditions of his curse. He remains alert to what he needs to remove the fairy's spell. He uses Positive Mental Attitude coupled with Definiteness of Purpose to move his plan forward, and he accomplishes his goal because he plans his work and works his plan. In the process, the magical advantages of establishing his mission coupled with a plan work on his behalf. His achievement occurs because he sees a better future for himself, he risks leaving the pond, and has a burning desire to be transformed back into his true self—the handsome Prince. The saying "Conceive It, Believe It, Achieve It" plays out once again in a picture-perfect end result!

++++++++++++++++++++++

Definiteness of Purpose with PMA
by Napoleon Hill & W. Clement Stone

Let us repeat: The starting point of all achievement is definiteness of purpose with PMA. Remember this statement and ask yourself, what is my goal? What do I really want?

Based on the people we see in our PMA Science of Success course, we estimate that 98 out of every 100 persons who are dissatisfied with their world do not have a clear picture in their mind of the world they would like for themselves.

Think of it! Think of the people who drift aimlessly through life, dissatisfied, struggling *against* a great many things, but without a clear-cut goal. Can you state, right now, what it is that you want out of life? Fixing your goals may not be easy. It may even involve some painful self-examination. But it will be worth whatever effort it costs, because as soon as you can name your goal; you can expect to enjoy many advantages. These advantages come almost automatically.

1. The first great advantage is that your subconscious mind begins to work under a universal law: "What the mind can *conceive* and *believe*—the mind can *achieve*." Because you visualize your intended destination, your subconscious mind is affected by this self-suggestion. It goes to work to help you get there.

2. Because you know what you want, there is a tendency for you to try to get on the right track and head in the right direction. You get into action.

3. Work now becomes fun. You are motivated to pay the price. You budget your time and money. You study, think, and plan. The more you think about your goals, the more enthusiastic you become. And with enthusiasm your desire turns into a *burning* desire.

4. You become alerted to opportunities that will help you achieve your objectives as they present themselves in your everyday experiences. Because you know what you want, you are more likely to recognize these opportunities.

Source: *Success Through A Positive Mental Attitude.* Prentice-Hall, Inc. 1960. Pgs. 24-25.

CHAPTER 21

*You can't depend on your eyes
when your imagination is out of focus.*
—MARK TWAIN

Who hasn't at one time or another wished they had a magic lamp? One just like Aladdin's that was home to a powerful genie housed inside. I bet even now you can picture the special lamp in your mind's eye and have at least ten items on your wish list that you would like fulfilled not now but RIGHT now. Thinking back to childhood, the story from the 1001 Tales of the Arabian Nights that inspired this reverie was none other than ***Aladdin & The Magic Lamp.*** Children read the story yet today in many versions. An updated version by John Patience is one that remains true to the original.

"Your Wish Is My Command!" The Genie of the lamp engages us all with that simple statement. And we like him instantly. Ironically, each of us has the same Genie inside the magic part of ourselves that we call the subconscious mind. We reach our subconscious mind through pure belief that is distilled by affirmations and habitual actions based on repeated choices. What we tell our subconscious minds continually throughout our lives and underscore with our habits, it believes and makes our every wish a command that appears in our lives. Pretty powerful genie.

Unfortunately, the lamp does not come with instructions nor does our subconscious mind. But wait! Once we learn how our mental genie works, we can call forth its magical results to insure our success. The formula R2 A2 that translates to RECOGNIZE, RELATE, ASSIMILATE, & APPLY works well in programming the lessons for success.

When Aladdin finds the magic lamp he doesn't know its capabilities. Likewise, when we discover our subconscious mind we are unsure how to engage its life changing properties. Through repetition and positive mental attitude we can learn to program our subconscious mind for desired results. Isn't it worth your time and effort to learn about this magical tool available to each and every one of us? You too can call forth the genie in your life and reap the rewards of knowing how to rub the lamp correctly to get the most optimum results.

✦✦✦✦✦✦✦✦✦✦✦✦✦✦✦✦✦✦✦✦✦✦

What Wouldst Thou Have?
by Napoleon Hill & W. Clement Stone

What wouldst thou have? "What wouldst thou have? I am ready to obey thee as thy slave—I and the other slaves of the lamp," said the genie.

Awaken the sleeping giant within you! It is more powerful than all the genii of Aladdin's lamp! The genii are fictional. Your sleeping giant is real.

What wouldst thou have? Love? Good health? Success? Friends? Money? A home? A car? Recognition? Peace of mind? Courage? Happiness? Or, would you make your world a better world in which to live? The sleeping giant within you has the power to bring your wishes into reality.

What wouldst thou have? Name it and it's yours. *Awaken the sleeping giant within you!* How?

Think. *Think with a positive mental attitude.*

Now the sleeping giant, like the genie, must be summoned with magic. But you possess this magic. The magic is your talisman, with the symbols PMA on one side and NMA on the other. The characteristics of PMA are the plus characteristics symbolized by such words as faith, hope, honesty, and love.

Source: *Success Through A Positive Mental Attitude.* Napoleon Hill & W. Clement Stone. Prentice-Hall, Inc. 1960. Pgs. 234-235.

PRINCIPLE 8

Enthusiasm

Enthusiasm is faith in action. Enthusiasm comes from the Greek words "en" which means "in" and "theos" which means "God." It is the intense emotion known as burning desire. Enthusiasm comes from within, although it radiates outwardly in the expression of one's voice and countenance. Enthusiasm is power because it is the instrument by which adversities and failures and temporary defeats may be transmuted into action backed by faith. The flame of enthusiasm burning within you turns thought into action.

CHAPTER 22

*Success is going from failure to
failure without loss of enthusiasm.*
    —SIR WINSTON CHURCHILL

During children's early years they have many imaginary adventures. These pretend happenings are enthusiastically embraced and can even develop into imaginary friends, imaginary tales of adventure, and imaginary journeys that place the child in the role of the main character or hero of the tale. These flights of fancy permit a youngster to wander into many different landscapes that would never occur in everyday life.

Opportunities to develop enthusiasm and even uncontrolled enthusiasm encourage boys and girls to try on different roles that may be eventually abandoned or hold lasting appeal for a latter day career choice.

How I Became a Pirate by Melinda Long and illustrated by David Shannon is an adventure on the high seas as imagined by Jeremy Jacob. While on a holiday with his family, Jeremy sees a pirate ship in the distance and then encounters the pirates in person as they row to shore. Looking for the Spanish Main the pirates take a wrong turn and end up at North Beach. Needing a mate to bury their treasure, 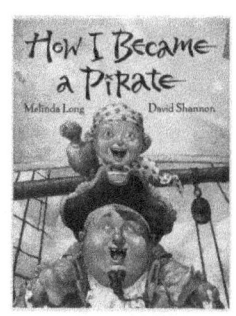 they add a willing Jeremy to their crew and haul him aboard. Jeremy is agreeable to the enlistment, as long as he is back for soccer practice the next day.

The story develops as Jeremy imagines the daily lives of the pirates in detail, but around bedtime Jeremy is missing his usual good night kiss, a good night story, and is lonesome for his parents. The tide literally turns as a storm develops, and Jeremy sees pirate life through enlightened eyes. It is decided that the treasure needs to be buried before the pirate ship can turn back to safety. Fortunately, Jeremy offers a practical solution and is able to return home with the treasure that he buries in his backyard. All the while, Jeremy learns through imaginary experience that a pirate's life can have both positive and negative aspects!

Think back and reimagine some of your childhood adventures. Did any turn out to embrace the career that you now hold as an adult? I bet in most cases parallels between what you enthusiastically imagined and what you are today have some similarities. So, in review, play aids in predetermining our outcomes. Play approached with enthusiasm allows children to try on certain roles before committing to these roles in reality. Play with enthusiasm can forecast what takes place in a child's future development. Take time today to encourage someone to develop the magic of enthusiastic play within and magic will surely happen for all to see on the outside too.

♦♦♦♦♦♦♦♦♦♦♦♦♦♦♦♦♦♦♦♦♦♦

Attract Happiness and Good Fortune
by Napoleon Hill

Remember, every person lives in two worlds: the world of his own mental attitude, which is greatly influenced by his associates and his surroundings, and the physical world in which he must struggle for a living. The physical world in which you make a living may be beyond your control, but you can, to a great extent, shape the circumstances of your immediate physical world. It can be done by the way you relate yourself to your mental world, for your mental attitude attracts to you those aspects of the physical world which harmonize with your mental attitude. Thus, pessimism will attract misery and ill fortune. But *enthusiasm,* properly controlled, will attract happiness and good fortune.

Enthusiasm is a great leavening force in your mental world, for it gives power to your purpose. It helps to free your mind of negative influences and brings you peace of mind. It wakens your imagination and stirs you to shape the circumstances of your physical world to meet your own needs.

But no amount of enthusiasm can replace *definiteness of purpose.* A man without a *definite major purpose* resembles a locomotive without a track to run on, or a destination toward which to travel. And if he lacks enthusiasm to back his *definite major purpose,* he is like a locomotive without fuel.

Enthusiasm may be expressed in two ways: *passively,* through the stimulation of emotional feeling which inspires you to meditate and think in silence; and *actively,* by the expression of such feeling through words and deeds.

Source: *PMA Science of Success.* Educational Edition. The Napoleon Hill Foundation. 1983. Pg. 250.

CHAPTER 23

Enthusiasm can only be aroused by two things: first, an ideal which takes the imagination by storm, and second, a definite, intelligible plan for carrying that ideal into practice.
—ARNOLD TOYNBEE

At times, enthusiasm evades us. We may feel sad, morose, or even fully depressed and unable to muster any feeling of positive energy for anything. This mood can only be lifted if we tell ourselves that to be enthusiastic we must act enthusiastically. The action of "forced" enthusiasm creates the emotion of enthusiasm. It is an outcome to a thought that we hold purposefully, with intention, in our mind. Many times before rallies and group meetings, W. Clement Stone and Napoleon Hill had the group recite memorized affirmations, auto-suggestions, and positive sayings in order to raise the energy in the room and also in the group. This works because when the mind tells the body that this is what is expected, the body confirms the command. The statement, "I feel healthy, I feel happy, I feel terrific!" recited with enthusiasm many times daily helps to make the statement true in reality. W. Clement Stone used this affirmation to live to be 100!

A children's book entitled ***The Secret Remedy Book*** by Karin Cates and illustrated by Wendy Anderson Halperin enlists the help of Auntie Zep in creating seven special remedies for niece Lolly who is overcome with loneliness, homesickness, and worry when she comes to spend some time with her Aunt Zep without her family. The "remedies" are simple adventures that they do together to pass the time and mend the heart. Simple actions such as planting a seed, feeding a wild thing, reading poetry, and drinking apple juice have profound ramifications that create a positive environment, then a comforting mood, and finally enthusism for the child who is missing her home and parents.

For example, the first remedy, sets the stage for adventure. It reads: "Drink one glass of apple juice. You must drink it so carefully that you can almost taste the very apple tree that made the apples that made the juice." The magic of enthusiasm is tastefully called to the scene and the stage is set for Auntie Zep and Lolly to anticipate the remaining six remedies together.

All said and done, enthusiasm can and should be cultivated. It can be called forth just as we hear in the command "Fake it until you make it!" We do not have to wait on enthusiasm to find us. Rather, we know the magical incantations that bring it forth and should use its power daily to enhance our well-being and the well-being of others we love and hold dear. Believe you can do it and your belief will make it so! Remedies are available to all of us. We just need to put the missing ingredients into action, and enthusism will sprout every single time.

✦✦✦✦✦✦✦✦✦✦✦✦✦✦✦✦✦✦✦✦✦✦

A Powerful Form of Energy
by Napoleon Hill

No one knows what thought is, but every philosopher and every man of scientific ability who has given any study to the subject is in accord with the statement that thought is a powerful form of energy which directs the activities of the human body; that every idea held in the mind through prolonged, concentrated thought, takes on permanent form and continues to affect the bodily activities according to its nature, either consciously or unconsciously.

Auto-suggestion, which is nothing more or less than an idea held in the mind, through thought, is the only known principle through which one may literally make himself over, after any pattern he may choose.

Source: *Napoleon Hill's Magazine.* July, 1921, Pg. 23.

CHAPTER 24

When enthusiasm is inspired by reason; controlled by caution; sound in theory; practical in application; reflects confidence; spreads good cheer; raises morale; inspires associates; arouses loyalty; and laughs at adversity, it is beyond price.
— COLEMAN COX

Granddad's Fishing Buddy written by Mary Quigley and illustrated by Stephane Jorisch is an example of the benefits of controlled enthusiasm. Staying overnight at her grandparents' cottage on the lake, Sara is so excited that she tries not to fall asleep because she doesn't want to miss a single moment of her holiday. Granddad is up very early and Sara decides to join him and asks "Why are you up?" He replies that he is going to meet his fishing buddy. Sara immediately asks to come too. Pausing for a moment, Granddad agrees.

Sara is overjoyed but soon learns that there are rules. She has to be real quiet. She has to be able to row the boat without making it turn in circles, and she has to be able to put a worm on a hook. Her excitement has to be contained, and she manages to control her enthusiasm in order to follow the rules. The fishing expedition exceeds Sara's expectations, and because she is a fast learner, she is invited to go fishing with Granddad again when she returns to the lake cottage.

Uncontrolled enthusiasm has been known to get people into trouble. Being too eager to plunge ahead without the other mediating traits of self-discipline, accurate thinking, and controlled attention cause many plans to go awry. Enthusiasm fuels our desires, but only a small bonfire may be necessary rather than a house fire to keep our flame of enthusiasm burning. Both children and adults need to learn just how much and when a display of enthusiasm is appropriate and beneficial. Learning that median point is very helpful because a little exuberance goes a long way. To be enthusiastic, act enthusiastic! But, remember to keep it low keyed in situations that require a quieter approach—such as fishing!

✦✦✦✦✦✦✦✦✦✦✦✦✦✦✦✦✦✦✦✦✦✦✦

Here's How We Do It!
by Napoleon Hill and W. Clement Stone

We call a student to the front of the class and give him a simple yet effective lesson that he will learn immediately. Here's how we do it—try it. Here is the dialogue that would take place between the instructor and student:
(Note: The dialogue of the instructor is in bold-face type. The student's answers are set in italics.)

Do you want to feel enthusiastic?
Yes.

Then learn the self-motivator: To be enthusiastic act enthusiastic. Now repeat this phrase.
To be enthusiastic act enthusiastic.

Right! What is the key word in the affirmation?
Act.

That's right. Let's paraphrase the message and thus you will learn the principle and be able to relate and assimilate it into your own life. If you want to be sick, what do you do?
Act sick.

You're right. If you want to be melancholy, what do you do?
Act melancholy.

Right again! And if you want to be enthusiastic, what do you do?
To be enthusiastic—act enthusiastic.

We then proceed to point out that you can relate this self-motivator to any desirable virtue or personal aim. Thus we might take justice as an example, and a card could read: To be just ACT just.

Source: *Success Through A Positive Mental Attitude.* Napoleon Hill and W. Clement Stone. Prentice-Hall, Inc. 1960. Pg. 121.

PRINCIPLE 9

Self-Discipline

Self-Discipline means taking possession of your own mind. Self-Discipline begins with the mastery of thought. If you do not control your thoughts, you cannot control your needs. Self-Discipline calls for a balancing of the emotions of your heart with the reasoning faculty of your head. It is the bottleneck through which all of your personal power for success must flow. Direct your thoughts, control your emotions, and ordain your destiny. As our culture has become more complex, the need for self-control has increased.

CHAPTER 25

*Action springs not from thought,
but from a readiness for responsibility.*
—DIETRICH BONHOEFFER

Self-Discipline is one of the most important principles in life to acquire and regulate. Without this character trait, nothing much gets accomplished. When teaching their children self-discipline, parents need to remember that this gift of self control combined with the idea of taking action for immediate and long term results is what determines outcome in life. Knowing why you discipline yourself and doing it daily is part of the process to self-actualization. Emotionally and rationally, self-discipline contributes to balance and satisfaction in life's journey. When you can credit your own ability in getting the job done, you gain a higher sense of self-esteem and go forward to achieve even more.

A beautiful book entitled *The Quilt Maker's Gift* by Jeff Brumbeau and illustrated by Gail de Marcken portrays this concept in an interesting manner. The old woman in this story is a master quilt maker, but only gives her quilts away when completed. The King hears of her masterpieces, and desires one of his own. Mandated to create a quilt for the King,  the old woman refuses saying that he needs to give everything he owns away before she will do this. Havoc follows, but the woman stands her ground. Finally, after much ranting and raving, the King decides to discipline himself in giving away some things. And then more, and finally almost everything. In the process he learns the joy of giving through self-discipline. As each possession is given away, the Quilt Maker adds another piece to the King's quilt. Finally, the King owns barely nothing because he has given everything away, but in the process he has earned the love of his subjects, and revels in the joy that he has brought to the people he now serves. The quilt nears completion, and the King is totally surprised and humbled when the old woman presents him with the most beautiful quilt in existence. He, in return, gives her his final possession—his throne. Together they make and distribute quilts to the poor of the land. Self-discipline enables both the old woman and the King to join forces for an even larger mission than either of them imagined. Envy, jealousy, self-righteousness, pride, and entitlement, all fall by the wayside when the true reason for living is discovered and applied. Being of genuine service to others is life's greatest reward. The King realizes that although he may now look poor, he is filled with all the memories of the happiness that he has created. His riches now exceed his own expectations!

When discussing this book with children, why not ask each boy or girl what special gift they can use to help others? Like the Quilt Maker's gift of quilting, each person feels an affinity to perhaps one or two special abilities. By pointing out how their gifts can be shared, each child will begin to imagine how this can be done within the home, school, neighborhood, and perhaps larger community. Expanding the vision of self through self-discipline enables seedling talents to grow and blossom into the very best gifts.

✦✦✦✦✦✦✦✦✦✦✦✦✦✦✦✦✦✦✦✦✦✦

Self-Mastery with Self-Discipline
by Napoleon Hill

Self-discipline entails the complete mastery of both your

thought habits and your physical habits. When you have gained control over your thought habits, control over your physical habits will be almost automatic, and you will be well on the road to the attainment of complete *self-discipline.*

The important fact to remember is that *self-discipline* calls for a balancing of the emotions of your heart with the reasoning faculty of your mind. This means that you must learn to consult both your feelings and your reason in reaching a decision concerning every circumstance of your life. Sometimes you will find it necessary to set aside your emotions entirely, and follow the dictates of your reason. Other times you will decide in favor of your emotions, modified by the advice of reason. Try to find the happy medium between too much and too little of everything.

For example, some men have so little control over the emotion of love that they are like so much putty in the hands of a woman. Such men never accomplish very much in life. And on the other hand there are the men who are emotionally cold because they follow completely and solely the advice of their minds.

Both of these types undoubtedly miss many of the finer things in life. The ideal is to achieve and maintain a proper balance between the faculties of reason and emotion. This is the highest form of *self-discipline.*

You may wonder if perhaps it would not be safer and wiser to control your life entirely on the basis of reason and leave emotion out of your decisions and plans. The answer to this question is: No. And it would be very unwise even if it were possible.

The emotions provide the driving power, the activating force, which enables a man to put the decisions of reason into action. The emotions are the well spring of man's greatest power. If you destroy hope and faith, what would there be to live for? If you kill enthusiasm, loyalty and the desire for achievement, but still retain the faculty of reason, what good will it be? The mind will still be there to direct, but what will it direct?

Source: ***PMA Science of Success.*** Educational Edition. The Napoleon Hill Foundation. 1981. Pgs. 269-270.

CHAPTER 26

*It takes time to succeed because success is merely
the natural reward of taking time to do anything well.*
—JOSEPH ROSS

Often our lives seem to run away with us. The winds of fate can and do blow us here and there if we fail to set a direct course for our preferred destination. As a ship without a set course or a pre-determined journey's end, a person can seemingly set sail in life but never reach any level of success because they have not charted a course and exerted self-discipline in planning to arrive at a certain port. Blown hither and yon, it seems as if life is predetermined, but the reality is, that is only true if we allow it to be. When an individual has a purpose and a plan that is enacted with self-discipline, even shooting for the moon is appropriate. Without a plan, a person usually lands somewhere, but generally not where he or she intended to be. Therefore, before embarking on any journey it is good to know the intended destination in advance. Other-wise, you may end up in a place that you least expected.

Daniel O'Rourke: An Irish Tale as told and illustrated by Gerald McDermott illustrates this point. Daniel is a fun-loving, jovial guy who parties hard and enjoys the fun that the great party at the mansion on the hill affords him. Walking home afterwards without a care or concern in  the world, he loses his footing on a slippery stone, and stumbles headlong into a rushing river that carries him out to sea. On his perilous journey he meets an eagle who flies him to the moon and leaves him there to dangle in the night sky. Next, the man in the moon encounters him and tells him that he must leave his home, and Daniel is cast adrift once again. Falling, Daniel remarks, "This is a pretty pickle for a decent man to be in." Next he encounters a flock of geese, and the head gander tells him to grab hold of his leg and he will fly him home. But, the goose flies past Daniel's little cottage and out to sea where he shakes him loose. Daniel plunges into the water, and fears for his life as he encounters a whale that bounces him up and down. Fearing the worst, Daniel awakens to his old mother throwing a bucket of water in his face and scolding him for falling asleep under the tower of a pooka, a magical creature in Irish fairy tales. A pooka often takes the shape of a horse and takes its victim on a wild ride that results in a true "night mare." Due to the frightful night, Daniel now agrees that he will watch his actions more in the future and never again fall victim to losing control. And, he decides to only sleep in his own bed from now on and not by the haunted tower.

This tale gives us insight into not taking control of our choices. By wandering willy-nilly down the cobblestone path of life, sometimes the slippery stones of poor decisions cast us adrift into a nightmare of unintended outcomes. But, by taking control of our thoughts and actions, we can be somewhat certain that our outcomes will be better than if we simply played the part of the fool and let whatever happens happen. Daniel O'Rourke is wiser for his encounters with the creatures who took him on a fantastic trip, and now he knows that he has to look out for the pitfalls that can occur when our best thoughts and corresponding good actions are not put in place before the journey begins.

++++++++++++++++++++++++

PUTTING THE PRINCIPLES INTO PRACTICE

Mastery of Your Thoughts
by Napoleon Hill

Self-discipline begins with the mastery of your thoughts. If you do not control your thoughts, you cannot control your deeds. Therefore, in its simplest form, *self-discipline* causes you to think first and act afterward. Almost everyone automatically does exactly the reverse of this. People generally act first and think later—unless they take possession of their minds and control their thoughts and deeds through *self-discipline.*

Self-discipline will give you complete control over fourteen major emotions listed below. Seven of these are positive, and seven negative:

Positive Emotions	Negative Emotions
a. Love	a. Fear
b. Sex	b. Jealousy
c. Hope	c. Hatred
d. Faith	d. Revenge
e. Enthusiasm	e. Greed
f. Loyalty	f. Anger
g. Desire	g. Superstition

All of these emotions are states of mind and are, therefore, subject to your control and direction. You can see instantly how dangerous the seven negative emotions can be if they are not mastered. The seven positive emotions can be destructive too, if they are not organized and released under your complete, conscious control. Wrapped up in these fourteen emotions is power of a truly explosive nature. If you regulate it properly, it can lift you to heights of distinguished achievement. But if you permit it to run rampant, it can dash you to pieces on the rocks of failure. You should realize that your education, your experience, your native intelligence and your good intentions cannot alter or modify these possibilities.

We have learned in previous lessons that a *definite major purpose, activated by a driving motive, is the starting point of all worthwhile achievement.* And this motive must be so strong that it will force you to subordinate all your thoughts and efforts to the attainment of your major definite purpose. But this drive must also be subject to the control of your own good judgment so that your enthusiasm and desire will not run away with your wisdom. In other words, you must discipline yourself so that your drive is at all times under control and directed in the proper channels.

Source: *PMA Science of Success.* Educational Edition. 1983. The Napoleon Hill Foundation. Pgs. 268-269.

CHAPTER 27

What we do upon some great occasion will probably depend on what we already are; and what we are will be the result of previous years of self-discipline.
—H.P. LIDDON

The Dance by Richard Paul Evans and illustrated by Jonathan Linton is the story of a daughter and her father. It details the moments in her life as she develops from a young girl who likes to play dress up into an accomplished ballerina who performs a solo in *The Nutcracker.* All the while, unseen, her father is watching and smiles as his daughter grows into a beautiful women who attends the prom, gets married,  and moves away. His memories of each of her special performances are forever preserved in photographs that he cherishes and looks at frequently.

Time moves forward, and the daughter is called home to visit her ill father. He asks her to dance for him again and she performs for him at the foot of the bed, and then because his sight has dimmed, she moves closer and grabs his hand and together they sway back and forth as if dancing. She tells him that no matter where she danced, she always danced for him. Now that he is dying, she tells him that she will not dance again. He quickly tells her that she must continue dancing because it is who she is and who he loves, and no matter where and when she dances he will always be watching and smiling.

This story of father and daughter requires the principle of

self-discipline because each is losing something special—each other. The father promises the daughter that he will always be watching her as she journeys through life, and the daughter has to believe this and continue to dance even after losing her inspiration and biggest admirer. Although bittersweet, the mutual realization is that life goes on despite the loss of loved ones. Life continues and giving up is not an option. Failures, disappointments, and losses occur for everyone. It is part of the cycle of life. Self-discipline requires that a person learn from these heartaches and look ahead, not behind. One's legacy should be a lesson in living and journeying on the path that is one of hope and faith. Fear looks back, and faith looks ahead.

Consider this story as a lesson in self-discipline. Some of the hardest lessons are those that enable us to grow in wisdom and understanding. Without self-discipline the lesson remains unlearned.

Door Closing
by Napoleon Hill

Consider the rather serious problems which arise in one's mind in connection with disappointments and failures of the past, and the broken hearts that occur as the result of the loss of material things or the loss of friends or loved ones.

Self-discipline is the only real solution for such problems, it begins with the recognition of the fact that there are only two kinds of problems: those you can solve, and those you can't solve.

The problem which can be solved should immediately be cleared by the most practical means available, and those which have no solution should be put out of your mind and forgotten.

Let us think, for a minute, about this process of forgetting. Refer to it as closing the door on some unpleasantness which is disturbing your emotional equilibrium. *Self-discipline*, which means mastery over all emotions, can enable you to close the door between yourself and the unpleasant experience of the past. You must close the door tightly and lock it securely, so that there is not possibility of its being opened again. This is the way to treat unsolvable problems, too. Those who lack self-discipline often stand in the doorway and look wistfully backward into the past, instead of closing the door and looking forward into the future.

This *door closing* is a valuable technique. It requires the support of a good, strong will, and you have a strong will if you have the departments of your mind organized and under the control of your ego, as they should be.

Door closing does not make you hard, cold or unemotional, but it does require firmness. *Self-discipline* cannot permit lurking memories of sad experiences, and it wastes no time worrying over problems which have no solution. You cannot yield to the temptation to relive your unhappy memories, for they destroy your creative force, undermine your initiative, weaken your imagination, disturb your faculty of reason, and generally confuse the departments of your mind.

You must place the power of your will against the door that shuts out that which you wish to forget, or you do not acquire self-discipline. This is one of the major services self-discipline can perform for you. It closes the door tightly against all manner of fears, and opens wide the doors of hope and faith!

Source: ***PMA Science of Success.*** Educational Edition. 1983. The Napoleon Hill Foundation. Pgs. 286-287.

PRINCIPLE 10

Accurate Thinking

The power of thought is the most dangerous or the most beneficial power available to man, depending, of course, upon how it is used. Through the power of thought man builds great empires of civilization. Through the same power other people trample down empires as if they were helpless clay. Thought is the only thing over which man has been given the complete privilege of control. The Accurate Thinker always submits his emotional desires and decisions to his head for judiciary examination before he relies upon them as being sound, for he knows that his head is more dependable than his heart. The accurate thinker separates facts from fiction and separates facts into two classes: important and unimportant.

CHAPTER 28

People only see what they are prepared to see.
—RALPH WALDO EMERSON

Seven Blind Mice written and illustrated by Ed Young is a good introduction to Accurate Thinking. According to Dr. Hill, the accurate thinker separates facts from fiction and separates facts into two classes: important and unimportant. In this children's story, the seven blind mice investigate the strange "something" by the  pond. Each sallies forth alone to determine what exactly the truth is. Six of the mice formulate conclusions on a part not the whole.

Red Mouse identifies the "something" as a pillar. Green Mouse identifies it as a snake. Yellow Mouse identifies it as a spear. Purple Mouse identifies it as a great cliff. Orange Mouse identifies it as a fan. Blue Mouse identifies it as a rope. But the seventh mouse, White Mouse, investigates the "something" thoroughly. She runs up one side and down the other, she runs across the top from end to end, and she collects, interprets, assimilates and synthesizes all the data.

After close analysis, White Mouse states: "The 'something' is as sturdy as a pillar, as supple as a snake, as wide as a cliff, as sharp as a spear, as breezy as a fan, and as stringy as a rope." Putting the details together, White Mouse concludes that the "something" is an elephant. Combining the data, the six other mice now "see" too. The moral of the story is: "Knowing in part may make a fine tale, but wisdom comes from seeing the whole."

Wisdom comes from seeing the whole picture, not just the individual parts. Dr. Hill states: The Accurate Thinker always submits his emotional desires and decisions to his head for judiciary examination before he relies upon them as being sound, for he knows that his head is more dependable than his heart.

Learning to be an Accurate Thinker requires dedicated time and work. The best way to get started is to always question ideas stated as fact. This can be done in a simple manner by asking the question "How do you know?" of the person making the declaration. Next, the person asking the question needs to check the source of the "factual" information for himself. This process aids in the separation of fact from opinion.

Always be ready to question a person's source of information. In this manner, you will then be better able to discern fact from fiction. Acquire this trait and your own thought process will be fine-tuned and more reliable with every decision you make. Sharpen the saw of your own thinking and improve your capacity for success!

✦✦✦✦✦✦✦✦✦✦✦✦✦✦✦✦✦✦✦✦✦

Clear the Cobwebs
by Napoleon Hill and W. Clement Stone

Cobwebs will interfere with accurate thinking and cause you to reach a wrong conclusion when you start with a false premise. W. Clement Stone had an amusing experience with this which he describes as follows:

As a boy I enjoyed eating frog legs. One day at a restaurant I was served jumbo frog legs and didn't like them. Then and there I decided that I didn't like large frog legs.

Some years later I was at a quality restaurant in Louisville, Kentucky and saw frog legs on the menu. My conversation with the waiter was as follows:

"Are these small frog legs?"
"Yes sir!"
"Are you sure? I don't like the large ones."
"Yes sir!"
"If they're the small ones, that'll be fine for me."
"Yes sir!"
When the waiter brought the entrée, I saw that they were jumbo frog legs. I was irritated and said: "These aren't the small frog legs!"

"These are the smallest we could find, sir," the waiter responded.

Rather than be unpleasant I ate the frog legs. And I enjoyed them so much that I wished they had been larger.

I learned a lesson in logic.

In analyzing the matter I realized that my conclusions about the merits of large and small frog legs had been based on the wrong premise. It wasn't the size of the frog legs that made them distasteful. It was the fact that the jumbo frog legs I had eaten the first time hadn't been fresh. I associated my distaste for jumbo frog legs with size rather than with spoilage.

Now we see that cobwebs prevent accurate thinking when we start with the wrong premise. So many persons think inaccurately when they allow all-embracing word symbols to clutter up their minds with false premises. Such words or expressions as: always—only—never—nothing—every—everyone—no one—can't—impossible—either...or—are most frequently false premises. Consequently, when they are so used their logical conclusions are false.

Source: *Success Through A Positive Mental Attitude.* Napoleon Hill & W. Clement Stone. Prentice-Hall, Inc. New Jersey. 1960. Pgs. 35-36.

CHAPTER 29

There must be more to life than having everything.
—MAURICE SENDAK

The Fisherman and His Wife is a classic fairy tale told by the Brothers Grimm. It is a tale about greed and the desire to have everything imaginable in life without earning it. The tale begins when a fisherman catches a large flounder that begs for his release. The fish tells the man that he is not really a flounder but an enchanted prince. Hearing his story, the man decides to let the talking fish go. Once back home,  the man relates the story to his wife, and she belittles him for his stupidity. She tells him to go and ask for a better home since they live in a hovel that is small and dirty. She concludes that if her husband caught an enchanted fish and let him go, the fish will grant the wish. Reluctantly, the fisherman returns to the sea and calls for the fish. The fish appears and grants the wife's wish. When he returns home, he finds his wife sitting on the front porch of a beautiful cottage. But within a few days, the wife is not satisfied, and wants even more. Her insatiable desire for more and more, requires that the fisherman return again and again to the sea with more requests that demand more elaborate gifts from the fish. The story ends on a sour note. The wife's final request is something that the fish chooses not to grant. Returning home, the fisherman finds that he and his wife have been returned to their hovel. She asked too much.

This tale can be interpreted from many levels. Let's look at it today through the lens of accurate thinking. Neither the fisherman nor his wife think accurately. The man fails to consider what his wife's requests really mean, and the wife only focuses on the ability of the fish to grant her every wish. Her arrogance, pride, greed, and every other personality disorder expand as she envisions greater and greater position in the world via only wishing and not earning. The husband follows along because he decides to keep the peace with his wife. They fail to think accurately. Since the husband is influenced by his wife, he tags along and has no desire of his own. He merely follows her lead. The wife sees the opportunity without the work and envisions a life that requires no dedication, work, or return on her part. In the end, the fish thinks more accurately than either of them.

Dr. Hill states: "Thousands of men and women carry inferiority complexes with them all through life, because some well-meaning but ignorant person destroyed their confidence through "opinions" or "ridicule." Truly, the wife is not even well-meaning, although she manages to destroy her husband's confidence through chastisement and ridicule. The wife epitomizes the concept that pride comes before the fall. Too much of anything is not a good thing, and the wife wants to have it all.

Consider how accurate thinking could have changed the outcome of this tale by the Brothers Grimm. What are other options that the fisherman and the wife could have taken to make the story end happily ever after? How will you now modify your decisions in life when you go fishing? Don't get hooked!

Tips on Making Your Own Decisions Using Accurate Thinking
by Napoleon Hill

The majority of people who fail to accumulate money sufficient for their needs are, generally, easily influenced by the opinions of others. They permit the newspapers and the gossiping neighbors to do their thinking for them. Opinions are the cheapest commodities on earth. Everyone has a flock of opinions ready to be wished upon anyone who will accept them. If you are influenced by opinions when you reach decisions, you will not succeed in any undertaking, much less in that of transmuting your own desire into money.

If you are influenced by the opinions of others, you will have no desire of your own.

Keep your own counsel, when you begin to put into practice the principles described here, by reaching your own decisions and following them. Take no one into your confidence, except the members of your "Master Mind" group, and be very sure in your selection of this group, that you choose only those who will be in complete sympathy and harmony with your purpose.

Close friends and relatives, while not meaning to do so, often handicap one through "opinions" and sometimes through ridicule, which is meant to be humorous. Thousands of men and women carry inferiority complexes with them all through life, because some well-meaning but ignorant person destroyed their confidence through "opinions" or ridicule.

You have a brain and mind of your own. Use it, and reach your own decisions. If you need facts or information from other people to enable you to reach decisions, as you probably will in many instances, acquire these facts or secure the information you need quietly, without disclosing your purpose.

Source: ***Think and Grow Rich.*** Ballantine Books. Random House. New York. 1983. Pgs. 120-121.

CHAPTER 30

We should know what our convictions are, and stand for them. Upon one's own philosophy, conscious or unconscious, depends one's ultimate interpretation of facts. Therefore it is wise to be as clear as possible about one's subjective principles. As the man is, so will be his ultimate truth.
—CARL JUNG

Who's afraid of the big, bad wolf? Well, we all should be if we have not used accurate thinking to determine his motives and the reason behind his solicitous nature. If the first two little pigs had prepared in advance, each may have realized the danger that was afoot and built their homes of brick instead of straw and sticks. The analogy is clear. Without accurate thinking what we may assume to be our best defense in really none at all. When someone comes along huffing and puffing all the while intending to do us harm, we may not be sufficiently prepared to withstand the situation and our houses will also tumble down.

The True Story of the 3 Little Pigs! by A. Wolf as told by Jon Scieszka and illustrated by Lane Smith, is Mr. Alexander T. Wolf's version of what really happened to the three little pigs. His story is far different from the one told by the reporters covering the homicides of the first two little pigs and Mr. Wolf's similar intention for number three. In this tale, he relates the true story, his version, of what really happened. With the evidence and the alibi placed side by side, whose story would you believe? Is

the wolf credible, and what might be his reasoning in presenting the facts as he sees them? How can we separate fact from fiction, and which facts are the important ones to consider in the outcome? Is Mr. Wolf really guilty, or are the pigs at fault for being inhospitable?

Most of us have seen many wolves in action. If we fall prey to their deceptions, who is to blame? Is it the wolf who is guilty, or is it also ourselves who allow the deception to occur? Easy prey makes easy victims. Our best defense is to learn how not to be victimized. By using the principle of accurate thinking, we may wind up not being eaten alive, but rather being the warden who oversees the wolf in the pig penn!

Consider Carl Jung's statement: "As the man is, so will be his ultimate truth." Look to a person's actions first, and not to his words. This is the best guide to the truth and integrity housed inside each of us. And wolves too!!

◆◆◆◆◆◆◆◆◆◆◆◆◆◆◆◆◆◆◆◆◆◆

Reminders to Yourself for Accurate Decision Making
by Napoleon Hill

It is characteristic of people who have but a smattering or a veneer of knowledge to try to give the impression that they have much knowledge. Such people generally do too much talking, and too little listening. Keep your eyes and ears wide open—and your mouth closed, if you wish to acquire the habit of prompt decision. Those who talk too much do little else. If you talk more than you listen, you not only deprive yourself of many opportunities to accumulate useful knowledge, but you also disclose your plans and purposes to people who will take great delight in defeating you, because they envy you.

Remember, also, that every time you open your mouth in the presence of a person who has an abundance of knowledge, you display to that person your exact stock of knowledge, or your lack of it! Genuine wisdom is usually conspicuous through modesty and silence.

Keep in mind the fact that every person with whom you associate is, like yourself, seeking the opportunity to accumulate money. If you talk about your plans too freely, you may be surprised when you learn that some other person has beaten you to your goal by putting into action ahead of you, the plans of which you talked unwisely.

Let one of your first decisions be to keep a closed mouth and open ears and eyes.

As a reminder to yourself to follow this advice, it will be helpful if you copy the following epigram in large letters and place it where you will see it daily: "Tell the world what you intend to do, but first show it."

Source: *Think and Grow Rich.* Ballantine Books. Random House. New York. 1983. Pg. 121.

PRINCIPLE 11

Controlled Attention

Controlled Attention leads to mastery in any type of human endeavor, because it enables one to focus the powers of his mind upon the attainment of a definite objective and to keep it so directed at will. Great achievements come from minds that are at peace with themselves. Peace within one's mind is not a matter of luck, but is a priceless possession, which can be attained only by Self-Discipline based upon Controlled Attention. Concentration on one's major purpose projects a clear picture of that purpose upon the conscious mind and holds it there until it is taken over by the subconscious mind and acted upon.

CHAPTER 31

*Concentration is everything. On the day I'm
performing, I don't hear anything anyone says to me.*
—LUCIANO PAVAROTTI

The Three Questions, written and illustrated by Jon J. Muth, is based on a story by Leo Tolstoy. In this children's version, Nikolai is seeking the answers to three questions from Leo, the wise old turtle. Nikolai's thoughtful questions are:

a. When is the best time to do things?
b. Who is the most important one?
c. What is the right thing to do?

As Nikolai sets out on his quest to find answers to his questions, he encounters someone needing help and someone in trouble. By acting on what needs to be done in the moment, he is led to the answers he seeks while on his own journey.

This philosophical story teaches that we find what we are seeking. By asking the questions and knowingly looking for answers, Nikolai is placing himself on the path of knowledge. He knows what he is looking for and recognizes it when he finds it. The clearer the vision, the more immediate and accurate the outcome. By using controlled attention in order to consciously look for a response, the subconscious mind is also engaged. When the outcome appears on schedule, it is recognized for what it is.

By being crystal clear in your mind as to your intended destination, distractions, blind alleys, and diversions can be avoided. The main ingredient in controlled attention is self-discipline. When a vision is created and self-discipline employed, the road to success is traveled more economically. Missteps are avoided and your course is charted toward success.

In the end of the story, the old turtle sums it up best by saying, "Remember then that there is only one important time, and that time is now. The most important one is always the one you are with. And the most important thing is to do good for the one who is standing at your side."

Wise words to live by. In summary, seek and you will find.

◆◆◆◆◆◆◆◆◆◆◆◆◆◆◆◆◆◆◆◆◆◆

The Key to Thought Power
by Napoleon Hill

Concentration on one's major purpose projects a clear picture of that purposes upon the conscious mind and holds it there until it is taken over by the subconscious and acted upon. This is called *controlled attention.*

Controlled attention is the act of coordinating all the faculties of the mind and directing their combined power to a given end. It is an act which can be achieved only by the strictest sort of self-discipline. Attention that is not controlled and directed may be nothing more than idle curiosity. The word *controlled* is the key to thought power.

You may achieve controlled attention by the application of the following six factors, through the application of *self-discipline:*

a. *Definiteness of purpose,* the starting point of all achievement.
b. *Imagination,* through which the object of one's purpose is illuminated and mirrored in the mind so clearly that

its nature cannot be mistaken.
c. *Desire,* turned on until it becomes burning desire that will not be denied.
d. *Faith* in the ultimate achievement of your purpose. This *faith* must be so strong that you can already see yourself in possession of the object of your *definite major purpose.*
e. *Will-power,* applied continuously, in full force, in support of faith.
f. The *subconscious mind* picks up the picture conveyed to it by the foregoing factors and carries it to its logical conclusion by whatever practical means may be available, according to the nature of your purpose.

Source: ***PMA Science of Success.*** Educational Edition. The Napoleon Hill Foundation. 1983. Pgs. 331-332.

CHAPTER 32

The world makes way for a man who knows where he is going.
                                        —RALPH WALDO EMERSON

One of the surest ways to practice controlled attention is to give thanks each day for all the goodness we have received during the past 24 hours. As we concentrate on the positive things in our lives, we push the negative things behind us and can move forward at a peaceful pace the next morning. As we concentrate on the good things that graced our day, we establish a pattern, a habit, that our subconscious minds can program into our system of operation. The saying, as within so without, enables us to act and replay the good things easily without additional effort.

With children this power can be easily developed through the practice of saying and memorizing daily prayers. The short morning prayer by Ogden Nash as quoted in Cyndy Szekeres' book, *A Small Child's Book of Prayers*, sets the stage for positive thoughts to begin an enjoyable day. It reads:

Now Another Day Is Breaking
Now another day is breaking,
Sleep was sweet and so is waking.
Dear Lord, I promised You last night
Never again to sulk or fight.
Such vows are easier to keep
When a child is sound asleep.
Today, O Lord, for Your dear sake,

I'll try to keep them when awake.
—OGDEN NASH

These thoughts upon waking, enable the child to focus on positive actions that he or she can control in order to make the day go better. If memorized and able to be recalled and verbalized upon command, the outcome is even greater since the child can correct an improper course of action when it is recognized. A parent, teacher, or another child may even assist in initiating the recall. So, there is a purpose and a plan for correction via the reminder of the prayer said in the morning.

The good night prayer serves as a capstone on the day just lived. Written by Henry Johnstone it reads:

Good Night Prayer
Bless my friends, the whole world bless,
Help me to learn helpfulness;
Keep me ever in Thy sight;
So to all I say good night.
—HENRY JOHNSTONE

By using these simple prayers with children, they will grow up with an arsenal of techniques in developing controlled attention that persists into adulthood. Simple prayers and positive thoughts enable children and adults to condition their minds with Positive Mental Attitude techniques that place them on the road to success at once or when they drift over to the negative side of life. Start early and remember that "thoughts are things." Thoughts always have and always will control our performance and outcome in life. Think and actualize good thoughts by using controlled attention!

Efficient Minds "FOCUS" Using Controlled Attention
by Napoleon Hill

The surest way of finding peace of mind is that which helps the greatest number of others to find it.

Let this be your guide to your use of the great motivating forces; then you will know you are using them correctly, not corrupting them.

Is there peace of mind in prayer? There can be. There *should* be. But note how many people go to prayer only in the hour of a misfortune, when the motive of *fear* dominates their minds. The approach must be negative in that case, and so, in terms of peace of mind, the results must be negative as well.

Prayers which bring peace of mind proceed from a mind which gives forth a confident message even though that mind may be afflicted with problems and sorrow. Prayers which free great forces to solve problems are born in minds which know that the problems can be solved once the forces are found—and have perfect confidence in the existence of those forces.

Along with many others I see evidence of an Intelligence beyond man's. I believe that the positively conditioned mind may at times tune in on that Intelligence. Yet mind-conditioning through prayer or resolution is something an individual must accomplish for himself. When the Creator made man free to see his own destiny, and choose between good and evil, he gave man this prerogative as well. Every great accomplishment of any man at any time first had to exist as a thought before it could exist in reality.

Source: ***Grow Rich With Peace of Mind.*** Ballantine Books. New York. 1996. Pgs. 45-46.

CHAPTER 33

The trouble with most people is that they quit before they start.
—THOMAS A. EDISON

Spiders and ants are things children pay attention to because of their industrious nature coupled with pure persistence. When outdoors, children watch their work with interest and attention. My grandson, Patrick, who has some learning setbacks can come up with confusing comments. Just recently upon viewing an ant, he commented to his mother:

Patrick: Mommy look at the ant, he is dead!

Me: (Surprised that he knew about death.) Dead? What does that mean? What's happening to the ant now that it is dead?

Patrick: He is going to burn in the sky.

Me: 8/—feeling confused. (Patrick's condition is described at: www.ocularmotorapraxia.org)

For me, it is fun as his grandmother to muse about what his insight may mean. I can't help think about Christianity, and how Christ often appears emblazoned in light. Could Patrick be associating the images of death and light in his young 4 year old mind? I hope so.

Stories like **The Itsy Bitsy Spider** as told and illustrated by Iza Trapani and songs like **High Hopes** made famous by Frank Sinatra promote the concepts of both controlled attention and hope through Applied Faith. Upon hearing these "story songs," children can begin to believe more in themselves and their potential that can lead to accomplishment through pure persistence, a characteristic of controlled attention.

Trials and tribulations confront the Itsy Bitsy Spider, but after keeping on keeping on, she reaches her goal. The last stanza in the song states:

> The itsy bitsy spider
> Climbed up without a stop.
> She spun a silky web
> Right at the very top.
> She wove and she spun
> And when her web was done,
> The itsy bitsy spider.
> Rested in the sun.

And, verses to High Hopes read:

> So any time your gettin' low
> 'Stead of lettin' go
> Just remember that ant
> Oops, there goes another rubber tree plant
> Oops, there goes another rubber tree plant
> Oops, there goes another rubber tree plant

I guess the message is that if an ant can do it, so can you! Control your attention, and control your outcome. Be persistent and at the most difficult moment the tide will turn in your favor and you will truly shine in a blaze of glory!

++++++++++++++++++++++

Turn the Tide with Controlled Attention
by Napoleon Hill

The combination, or connection between the individual minds, is achieved through the principle of *controlled attention*, concentrated effort, wherein each individual subordinates his personal desires for the benefit of the group.

This is the way the *master mind* principle works. It is the secret of all great achievements, whether they are achievements of industry, religion, education, statesmanship, warfare or otherwise. The *master mind* principle is the way to great mind power—the kind of power required for all great achievements.

> *You can't control other men's actions,*
> *but you can control your mental reaction*
> *to their acts and that is what counts most to you.*

We repeat this truth for the sake of emphasis, for it is the key to this entire philosophy.

Controlled attention leads to mastery in any type of human endeavor, because it enables one to focus the powers of his mind upon the attainment of a definite objective and to keep it so fixed at will. *Controlled attention* is self-mastery of the highest order, for it is an accepted fact that the man who controls his own mind may control everything else that gets in his way.

It was this sort of control which Harriet Beecher Stowe had in mind when she said:

> *When you get into a tight place and everything goes against you, 'til it seems as though you could not hold on a minute longer, never give up then, for that is just the place and time that the tide will turn.*

The tide seems always to turn in your favor if you are determined to see that it does. Your state of mind has everything to do with turning the tide. Plato expressed this thought in his statement:

> *The first and best victory is to conquer self; to be conquered by self is, of all things, the most shameful and vile.*

Francis Parkman showed his understanding of the power of the mind, and particularly the power available through controlled attention, when he wrote:

> *He who would do some great thing in this short life must*

apply himself to work with such concentration of his forces as, to idle spectators, who live only to amuse themselves, looks like insanity.

Washington Irving expressed his respect for the power of the mind in these words:

Great minds have purposes, others have wishes. Little minds are turned and subdued by misfortune; but great minds rise above them.

Source: ***PMA Science of Success Course.*** Educational Edition. The Napoleon Hill Foundation. 1983. Pgs. 333-334.

PRINCIPLE 12

Teamwork

Teamwork is harmonious cooperation that is willing, voluntary and free. Whenever the spirit of Teamwork is the dominating influence in business or industry, success is inevitable. Harmonious cooperation is a priceless asset that you can acquire in proportion to your giving. Teamwork, in a spirit of friendliness, costs little in the way of time and effort. Generosity, fair treatment, courtesy, and a willingness to serve are qualities that pay high dividends whenever they are applied in human relations.

CHAPTER 34

It takes two flints to make a fire.
—LOUISA MAY ALCOTT

Together... We can by Beth Shoshan and Petra Brown is a simply written children's book about doing and learning things together. Two characters "Big" for big bear and the narrator who is a little koala bear, romp and play together. Big shows the baby koala how to do things and baby koala tries to imitate him. But, being small, baby koala can only do small versions of the great feats performed by Big.  Going alone, baby koala finds that he too can do many things that Big cannot do. Surprisingly he enjoys these things less because they are not done together. He concludes that whatever each of them can do, they are better doing things together.

The lesson is simple. Knowledge is shared and passed on to the next generation in a free flowing and enjoyable manner. It is okay to go it alone, but better to go it together. The acts that are performed by Big serve as instruction and legacy for the next generation. Time spent with each other solidifies the bonds between generations and serves as a tool for building community, continuity, and connectivity.

Napoleon Hill discusses this in his writings. He states: "Not only does your present and future depend upon your ability to join hands with others—but the tomorrow our children will know will depend upon how willing we are to walk the road of life together in peace and prosperity as we build a better world."

The saying "Teamwork Makes the Dream Work" is a good motto for making the world a better place in which to live through teamwork. The process begins early with simple activities done in childhood. Engagement and participation enable children to experience the fun and joy in cooperative efforts that transfer over to adulthood. It is not competition but communication through teamwork that will enable the world to become better.

Why not participate in teamwork work right now? Share something with your child today and these activities will pay high dividends tomorrow. Go ahead. Make a difference!

◆◆◆◆◆◆◆◆◆◆◆◆◆◆◆◆◆◆◆◆◆

Be a Bridge Builder
by Napoleon Hill

Cooperation, like love and friendship, is something you get by giving.

There are many travelers on the road that leads to happiness. You will need their cooperation, and they will need yours.

And there will be other generations after ours. Their lot in life will depend largely on the inheritance we leave to them. We must become bridge-builders, not only for the present generation but for generations yet unborn. And we must build for them in the spirit of the old man about whom the poet wrote:

The Bridge Builder
By Will Allen Dromgoole

An old man going a lone highway,
Came, at the evening cold and gray,
To a chasm vast and deep and wide.

Through which was flowing a sullen tide
The old man crossed in the twilight dim,
The sullen stream had no fear for him;
But he turned when safe on the other side
And built a bridge to span the tide.

"Old man," said a fellow pilgrim near,
"You are wasting your strength with building here;
Your journey will end with the ending day,
You never again will pass this way;
You've crossed the chasm, deep and wide,
Why build this bridge at evening tide?"

The builder lifted his old gray head;
"Good friend, in the path I have come," he said,
"There followed after me to-day
A youth whose feet must pass this way.
This chasm that has been as naught to me
To that fair-haired youth may a pitfall be;
He, too, must cross in the twilight dim;
Good friend, I am building this bridge for him!"

Source: ***Father: An Anthology of Verse*** (EP Dutton & Company, 1931)

This spirit of unselfish team work will provide greater benefits for this generation, as well as help those yet to come. Thus, in serving as bridge-builders for future generations we shall be preparing ourselves for the better things of life which can come only through friendly cooperation.

If you use this philosophy for personal benefit, remember you owe something to those who will follow you. Remember, too, to build for them.

Source: ***PMA Science of Success Course.*** Educational Edition. The Napoleon Hill Foundation. 1983. Pgs. 355 & 356.

CHAPTER 35

*It marks a big step in a man's development when
he comes to realize that other men can be called
in to help him do a better job than he can do alone.*
—ANDREW CARNEGIE

Don Quixote and Sancho Panza are the perfect example of teamwork. In the work by Miguel de Cervantes entitled ***Don Quixote of La Mancha,*** Cervantes has written a classic, universal tale that maintains its appeal worldwide. When read, the story of the faithful knight and his worthy assistant engage the reader. As they travel along on their quest, we accompany them in spirit. Their purpose  in righting the wrongs of the world invites readers to join forces with them and travel along. When goodness is the banner cry of the campaign, it seems correct to follow their lead. It has been said that this novel should be read at least three times in a person's life: beginning, middle, and end. Why? Because wisdom grows as we mature and what could be viewed in our youth as a silly story about a deranged old man and his stupid sidekick can change into a metaphor for our life's work. Whether it's mission accomplished, or mission abandoned remains to be seen.

The irony at the end of the novel is that when Don Quixote is forced to see "reality," he returns to sanity and dies feeling that he failed. But, for those in the team whom he touched with his "impossible dream," his vision survives and propels both

Sancho Panza and Aldonza alias Dulcinea into continuing the mission. As they are changed by their relationship to Don Quixote and his lofty values, so too can we be made aware of how "impossible" turns into "possible." Wisdom is earned by degrees, and advancement in life is attained by the journeys completed.

Multiple versions of this story can be introduced to children. One that remains close to the original is the one adapted by Margaret Hodges. In this compilation she introduces children to stories taken from the novel, such as "A Knight Rides Forth," "The Battle with the Windmills," and "Sancho's Story." Once accustomed to the characters and their escapades, children might also enjoy seeing the musical, **Man of La Mancha**, which features the well-known song, *The Impossible Dream*. Insight can grow with each addition.

Frequently, Dr. Hill discusses the *Twelve Riches of Life*. Each of the traits describes Don Quixote as he lives out his mission. When a person has a compelling dream and pursues that dream with all his heart, it seems entirely reasonable that the *Twelve Riches of Life* show up right on schedule. As you read the story with a child, remember to ask "What is your dream?" I predict that you will be surprised at some of the responses you hear. Encourage the young dreamer to dream with abandon, and never give up finding how that dream can meet reality if enough time, energy, and action are mingled with the desires and creative vision that can bring it forth for the betterment of the entire team. Remember, teamwork makes the dream work.

Why not participate in teamwork right now? Share something with your child today and these activities will pay high dividends tomorrow. Go ahead. Make a difference!

The Spirit of Teamwork
by Napoleon Hill

Success in life is made up of many little circumstances which most people never recognize as being of value to themselves. Failure likewise is made up of small circumstances which go unnoticed by those who fail. A great industrialist once said: *Friction in machinery is costly, but friction in the relationships of men who operate machinery is fatal—both to themselves and their associate workers.*

Team work in a spirit of friendliness costs so little in the way of time and effort, and it pays such huge dividends not only in money but in the finer things of life. One wonders why so many people go out of their way to make life miserable for themselves and others by failure to recognize this truth. A kindly word here, a kindly deed there, a pleasant smile everywhere, and this world would be a better place for all mankind.

This is the spirit which lights the path to Happy Valley for all who adopt it. And it is the spirit which leads to the attainment of the twelve riches of life: a *positive mental attitude,* sound physical health, harmony in human relationships, freedom from fear, the hope of achievement, the capacity for faith, a willingness to share one's blessings, a labor of love, an open mind on all subjects, *self-discipline,* the capacity to understand people, and last but not least, economic security. What an array of riches, and each of them tied in with that little phrase *team work!*

Source: ***PMA Science of Success Course.*** Educational Edition. The Napoleon Hill Foundation. 1983. Pgs. 361 & 362.

CHAPTER 36

*It is not fair to ask of others what
you are not willing to do yourself.*
—ELEANOR ROOSEVELT

Teamwork enables us to join forces with many people for superior results. Think of an orchestra, a band, a school, a community, a church, or even a club. They all function due to the concept of teamwork. Without a team, none of these organizations would exist in and of themselves. While each of us strives to do our best in contribution to the whole, each of us cannot do it all. It takes a team to build something lasting, worthwhile and unique. Any structure maintains its integrity by the competent and varied contributions of each member.

Just think of a band. Singly each person may be a strong musician; however, individually they cannot both put on a show and play the selections simultaneously. A professional worker handling the lighting, sound system and stage are required for the performance. And, most importantly so is the audience. Just begin to consider all the component parts of a production and you have the staggering idea of how monumental a task it can be to make even the simplest performance occur. Why? Because each of us has our role to perform, and we do best by sharing our talent and then asking for cooperation and assistance in areas wherein we are lacking. Teamwork is a much required asset in making our dream come true.

In an informative book called **Meet the Orchestra** by Ann Hayes

and illustrated by Karmen Thompson, children are introduced to the instruments played in an orchestra. Not only is this educational, but it presents children the opportunity to see how instruments can be played alone or together. When combined in a performance, each instrument contributes to the outcome produced by every one of the performers. Surely, in this circumstance there is no "I" in team. All members including the conductor blend into one harmonious whole.

This weekend I attended several performances at a music fest. All of the bands were good, but I always look forward to hearing my favorite. This time however, one of the quartet was ill. As he told the audience at the beginning of the performance, he caught something crossing over the pond and was not himself. Other things went amiss too. The audio was off, the neighboring performance was very loud and their sound leached over into the band's space, and finally an overly enthusiastic, although friendly, fan refused to take his seat. Exasperation crept over the band member's faces, and it was apparent that this was not going to be their best performance. It was hard for them to continue, but they did. They played through all of the mishaps and performed for over one hour and thirty minutes. They concluded to two standing ovations. Was it their best performance? No. But the fans responded because the band performed. Neither gave up. Each supported the other as a team, and in the end a sincere "thank you" came from both sides of the stage with a promise from the band to do better the next night.

I have heard it stated that it is okay to fail. With each consecutive attempt, we just have to learn to fail better. The performance could have been cancelled, a scene could have been made over the fan who would not sit down, or the ill performer could have left the show to the remaining three, but the band stuck together as a family. Herein lies a better lesson than how to give a brilliant performance. The lesson I witnessed was, sink or swim we are all in this show together. We can fail, or we can make our best attempt at doing our very best. Even then, we can fail but at least we won't be labelled quitters. By the way, the final two songs were exceptional. The audience sent their energy to the band, and the band bounced back to deliver their best performance right on schedule.

Lesson learned: When we do not worry about who gets the credit, everyone shares in the glory.

✦✦✦✦✦✦✦✦✦✦✦✦✦✦✦✦✦✦✦✦✦

Friendly Team Work
by Napoleon Hill

Everywhere and in everything friendly team work is a fundamental principle of growth and power. Nature is our authority for the soundness of this principle. Our body, for example, is one of nature's most remarkable demonstrations of the power and value of team work.

The body consists of countless billions of cells, each of which serves a definite purpose in connection with the growth and maintenance of the whole. These cells are organized into groups known as organs, such as the heart, lungs, liver, brain, spinal cord, alimentary canal, veins and nerves. Each organ has its specific work to do. When one fails, the entire pattern is disrupted and some form of physical disorder follows.

Team work also plays an essential part in music. Harmony of voices in a choir, the blended tones of many musical instruments in an orchestra or band, are achieved through practiced coordination of effort: team work.

A successful play can be produced only by careful cooperation of the players, the director, the stage hands and everyone connected with the project.

The game of bridge provides another excellent example of the value of team work. And it is the absolute rule in the great American games of football, baseball and basketball.

Throughout life every great victory is supported by some kind of friendly team work. Sometimes the wearer of the crown of success owes their victory to the unselfish team work of their spouse; sometimes to an efficient secretary or business partner, or to a group of loyal associate workers who help him to carry out his plans. It is a mark of great wisdom when any man displays skill in winning the friendly cooperation of his associates.

Source: *PMA Science of Success Course.* Educational Edition. The Napoleon Hill Foundation. 1983. Pgs. 373 -374.

PRINCIPLE 13

Learning from Adversity and Defeat

Every adversity carries with it the seed of an equivalent or greater benefit. Individual success usually is in exact proportion to the scope of the defeat the individual has experienced and mastered. Most so-called failures represent only a temporary defeat that may prove to be a blessing in disguise. Defeat is never the same as failure unless and until it has been accepted as such.

CHAPTER 37

Those things that hurt, instruct.
—BENJAMIN FRANKLIN

When a sadness enters our lives, it can become an opportunity to learn from Adversity and Defeat. Bad news, disappointments, losses, tragedies, and nameless things that seem insurmountable in our lives can lead to positive outcomes if the process of grieving is given the chance to bring us through the situation into a new way of being alive. As we grieve, we learn, and as we learn we discover that life can and will go on with or without us.

A book for all ages by Pat Schwiebert and Chuck DeKlyen, and illustrated by Taylor Bills is suited for a rainy day (or month or year) of the heart. It is entitled *Tear Soup: A Recipe for Healing After Loss.* The type of loss is not important, except for the fact that the loss is something that the person needs to grieve in order to continue to live and to heal beyond the loss.

The authors discuss **Tear Soup** by explaining:

Some cooking requires that you measure ingredients exactly.
But making soup is different.
Soup making is an art, and you are the artist.
Improvising as you go, your only goal
is that the blended creation will both
satisfy your hunger and soothe what hurts you.

> "What's true about soup making,
> is also true about grieving."

Learning about the process of grieving can assist us with looking ahead for the equal or equivalent benefit that accompanies the loss. Knowing that the benefit is there waiting for us even if it is invisible at the moment, allows a ray of light to enter into our darkness. A single flicker of a candle can illuminate the darkness of loss, and that is what is needed in order to begin to come back to life. Our losses are unique and best understood by ourselves. The process of reversing losses takes time, effort, understanding and grieving over what was but is no longer. When adversity and defeat enter our lives, our lives are not over but something that we cherish has come to an end. It is now our opportunity to honor the memory and move forward in a way that heals the hurt but never diminishes the love that came before. Know that by making Tear Soup you will be preparing to live again in a new way with wisdom earned from the experience. For right now, that simple nourishment could be enough to get you started on the road to healing.

✦✦✦✦✦✦✦✦✦✦✦✦✦✦✦✦✦✦✦✦✦✦

Shadows of Mournful Regrets
by Napoleon Hill

Every adversity has within it the seed of an equivalent or a greater benefit. Can you remember that? Write it on a card. Carry the card in your pocket and read it daily! In that phrase lies the key to many a man's peace of mind. It is not the Supreme Secret to which I have referred but it lives on the same street. Set it firmly into your consciousness: *Each adversity has within it the seed of an equivalent or a greater benefit.*

Thus it is possible, and strongly advisable, to **CLOSE THE DOORS TO YOUR PAST** insofar as any regrets or bitterness or post-mortems are concerned. You are searching for wealth and peace of mind. Neither the way to wealth nor the way to peace of mind leads through the graveyard of unpleasant experiences long past.

When you have attained peace of mind, your mind will automatically reject every thought and every mental reaction which is not beneficial to your welfare. Meanwhile, help yourself attain this great command-of-mind and all it can do for you. Avoid all negative mental influences and especially avoid that shadow of mournful regret which can keep all the sunshine out of your life—and keep out other gold as well.

Source: *Grow Rich! With Peace of Mind.* Ballantine Books. Trade Edition. 1996. Pg. 21.

CHAPTER 38

Problems are the cutting edge that distinguishes between success and failure. Problems...create our courage and wisdom.
—M. SCOTT PECK

Words and thoughts can be positive or negative. They can even ricochet, rebound, or boomerang back to the speaker. This cycle creates either good or bad results depending upon what was initially spoken into existence. Thinking that words have no effect and can never hurt or heal a person is nonsense. Words pack tremendous power to heal or harm, and caution needs to be taken in how words are spoken, or even thought. "In the beginning was the word," is true for every creative act that sees the light of day in our dimension of living. Words do create our Universe.

A good friend told me that she can just look at a person and sense the emotion that they are feeling by how they appear at the moment. Being sad, happy, annoyed, or displeased begins with a thought, and the thought translates into an emotion that can be "read" on a person's face. Without saying a word, we can see what they are thinking. "Thoughts are things," as Napoleon Hill reminds us.

Good and bad things can happen that determine future outcomes. A little story by Sam McBratney and illustrated by Jennifer Eachus entitled *I'm Sorry* shows this process at work. Two children are the best of friends until one day they shout at each other, and their friendship ends. Each is hurt by

the words the other spoke. They stay apart, but miss each other. Finally, the idea of saying "I'm sorry" is offered as a way to mend the friendship. If spoken, the little boy and girl may soon forgive and forget, and the friendship can be renewed.

The learning here is that words can cause serious changes in relationships. Even when "I'm sorry" is spoken, the hurt can still linger in our subconscious and conscious minds. People become more cautious and less outgoing. If you are unsure, your thoughts need to remain just that—thoughts, not words. Unfortunately, forgive and forget isn't always the exact formula that follows a breakdown in communication. Prevent a potentially negative outcome by considering what you intend to say before you say it. Words are many things to many people depending upon the intention behind them. Make your intention a good one!

◆◆◆◆◆◆◆◆◆◆◆◆◆◆◆◆◆◆◆◆◆◆

The Disaster of Destructive Thinking
by Napoleon Hill

The person who gives expression, by word of mouth, to negative or destructive thoughts is practically certain to experience the results of those words in the form of a destructive "kick-back." The release of destructive thought impulses, alone, without the aid of words, produces also a "kick-back" in more ways than one.

First of all, and perhaps most important to be remembered, the person who releases thoughts of a destructive nature must suffer damage through the breaking down of the faculty of creative imagination.

Secondly, the presence in the mind of any destructive emotion develops a negative personality which repels people, and often converts them into antagonists.

The third source of damage to the person who entertains

or releases negative thoughts lies in this significant fact—these thought impulses are not only damaging to others, but they imbed themselves in the subconscious mind of the person releasing them, and there become a part of his character.

Your business in life is, presumably, to achieve success. To be successful, you must find peace of mind, acquire the material needs of life, and above all, attain happiness. All of these evidences of success begin in the form of thought impulses.

Source: *Think and Grow Rich.* Ballantine Books. 1983. Pg. 221.

CHAPTER 39

The successful person is the individual who forms the habit of doing what the failing person doesn't like to do.
—DONALD RIGGS

Is today already carved out to be "one of those days?" Did you wake up to spoiled coffee cream, a bill you forgot to pay, a missed hair appointment, dirty dishes in the sink, a cat who just missed the litterbox by three inches, bad news in an email, more constantly bad news on CNN, a complaining spouse, a co-worker who calls off and leaves you with a big project deadline, a sick friend, and...the litany goes on and on. With that list of negativities, who in their right mind would want to open the front door and cross the threshold to face an even bigger onslaught in the outside world?

But, isn't that approximately the list that many of us face each day? As we ready ourselves for more of the negative occurrences we may fall under the belief that someone has cast a bad spell on us! But enough! What's missing is our focus. What needs to be done is a realignment of our attitude in order to cast out the awareness of the "bad" and usher in an awareness of the "good." In all circumstances, it can be done, and you can do it IF you consciously realign your vision upon awakening with making it a good news instead of a bad news day. You create your world by your response to it. And, be aware that the focus you take is contagious and can just as easily spread to others around you too.

In the classic children's story by Judith Viorst, ***Alexander and the Terrible, Horrible, No Good, Very Bad Day,*** everything bad happens to Alexander. He steps in gum, there is no dessert in his lunchbox, he fights with his brother, and on and on. He expects the worst and it lines up minute by minute to meet his expectation. His conclusion is that it would be better in Australia, and he thinks about moving there. We all know that it is not the physical move, but the inside move that will help Alexander experience a more  positive day. When he wakes up with a negative attitude coupled with a negative intention to experience the worst, it happens right on schedule just as he knew it would.

A project that can be done with this story for children of all ages is to rewrite the story from a positive frame of reference. Each incident can be taken and reconstructed for a positive outcome so as to find the benefit in the adversity. By looking at how thought can turn a bad day into a good day, we begin to see our control over each and every outcome in our lives. Alexander's Horrible Day can refocus into Alexander's Exemplary Day with a twist of focus. Try it and see for yourself. Retrain your thought, adjust your focus, look for the good in everything, and begin to make your dreams come true rather than be subject to a nightmare of your own creation.

✦✦✦✦✦✦✦✦✦✦✦✦✦✦✦✦✦✦✦✦✦✦

Positive Qualities of Defeat
by Napoleon Hill

A man's mental attitude in respect to defeat is the factor of major importance in determining whether he rides with the tides of fortune on the success side of the River of Life or is swept to the failure side by circumstances of misfortune.

The circumstances which separate failure from success often are so slight that their real cause is overlooked. Often they exist entirely in the mental attitude with which one meets temporary defeat. The man with a *positive mental attitude* reacts to defeat in a spirit of determination not to accept it. The man with a negative mental attitude reacts to defeat in a spirit of hopeless acceptance.

The man who maintains a *positive mental attitude* may have anything in life upon which he may set his heart, so long as it does not conflict with the laws of God and the rights of his fellowmen. He probably will experience many defeats, but he will not surrender to defeat. He will convert it into a stepping stone from which he will rise to higher and higher areas of achievement.

The subject of a *positive mental attitude* is so important that it not only claimed first position in the list of the twelve riches of life, but it had to be included as an important part of the principle on *pleasing personality,* and has been mentioned in practically every principle of this course.

A *positive mental attitude* is an essential part of the key which unlocks the door to the solution of all personal problems. It is the magic quality of this key which enables it to attract success as surely as an electro-magnet attracts iron filings.

The whole secret of the formula by which you may turn defeat into an asset lies in your ability to maintain a *positive mental attitude* despite your defeat.

Source: ***PMA Science of Success.*** Educational Edition. The Napoleon Hill Foundation. 1983. Pgs. 395-396.

PRINCIPLE 14

Creative Vision

Creative Vision is developed by the free and fearless use of one's imagination. Creative Vision attains its ends by basically new ideas and methods. It is not a miraculous quality with which one is gifted or is not gifted at birth. It is a quality that may be developed. It may be an inborn quality of mind, or an acquired quality, for it may be developed by the free and fearless use of the faculty of imagination. Our country needs Creative Vision now as it has never needed it before.

CHAPTER 40

Nothing happens unless first a dream.
—CARL SANDBURG

Have you ever had an idea follow you around and pester you to pay attention to it? Maybe you named your idea, or came to treat it as a daily companion, or even tried to make it go away. Regardless, it stayed like a stray dog that appeared on your doorstep one day and called you master. Ideas can be like that, and when they claim you, you have to feed them with whatever it takes to satisfy their craving to see the light of day.

I have heard some people say, "this idea won't leave me alone." I have watched people protect their ideas and never let them "grow up." These ideas are coddled and spoiled so that they never mature. These idea caregivers fear that their baby ideas may dissolve and perish if released. After all, they are "my" ideas, right?

The reality is that our ideas are there waiting to be born. Their gestation period is irregular. It could be nine months or nine years or even nine decades, but the ideas inside of us want to be born into the world. They are our ideas, but they are placed inside of us to share and not to be jailed under lock and key.

The children's book ***What Do You Do With An Idea?*** written by Kobi Yamada and illustrated by Mae Besom makes an Idea come to life. This is a book for all ages to read. It inspires and explains what you do with an idea. In allowing it to grow and giving it the environment that it needs to transform itself into something special, you "gift" your idea to the world. By setting an idea free you learn that it can now be part of everything for everyone. It parallels Dr. Hill's mantra of "Conceive it, Believe it, Achieve it." One idea at a time, freed up, can indeed change the world.

What will you do with your idea? Why not release it and see if it can make the world a better place in which to live? Could it be that your idea is the idea whose time has come? Find out.

✦✦✦✦✦✦✦✦✦✦✦✦✦✦✦✦✦✦✦✦✦

The Free and Fearless Use of the Imagination
by Napoleon Hill

Creative vision, expressed by men and women who have been unafraid of criticism has been responsible for the civilization of today as we know it. It has also been responsible for the scientific inventions of modern times which have led first to the steamboat age during the days of Robert Fulton; then the railroad age, the electrical age, the steel and iron age, the department store age, the skyscraper age, the automobile age, the airplane age, the age of plastics, and finally the atomic and space age.

Creative vision inspires men to pioneer and to dare to experiment with new ideas in every field of endeavor. It is always on the lookout for a better way of doing man's labor and supplying man's needs.

Creative vision is a quality of mind belonging only to men and women who follow the habit of going the extra mile, for it recognizes no such thing as the regularity of working hours, is not concerned with monetary compensation, and its highest aim is to do the impossible.

This quality, more than all others, gave us Thomas Jefferson, Benjamin Franklin, Thomas Paine, George Washington,

Abraham Lincoln and many other great statesmen who laid the solid foundation for our way of life.

And it gave us Thomas A. Edison in invention, Henry Ford in automobile transportation, Orville and Wilbur Wright in the development of the airplane, James J. Hill in railroad pioneering, F. W. Woolworth in chain store merchandising, Andrew Carnegie in the development of the steel industry, Charles M. Schwab in the same industry, John D. Rockefeller, Sr., in the refinement of crude oil, and many other American industrialists who pioneered our system of free enterprise through the trail and error method, and developed it to the point at which it is today.

Creative vision may be an inborn quality of the mind, or it may be an acquired quality, for it may be developed by the free and fearless use of the faculty of the *imagination*.

Source: **PMA *Science of Success.*** Educational Edition. The Napoleon Hill Foundation. 1983. Pg. 401.

CHAPTER 41

If you have built castles in the air, your work need not be lost; that is where they should be. Now put the foundations under them.
—HENRY DAVID THOREAU

Have you ever thought about what Da Vinci, Michelangelo, Mother Teresa, Cousteau, Lincoln, Florence Nightingale, and others whose names today are household words played at as children? In years gone by, were there imaginary canvases, treasure hunts, carvings, teachings, court rooms, and hospital beds that positioned them for their lifelong work? Think back on your own early years and see if you can identify a slender thread, maybe even a rope, that you created and held on to that became your bowline, your tether, into your future role as an adult. Makes you sense sometimes that what you dream about you become, right? Right.

When I think back on my childhood, it was filled with books, dolls, and cats that became a makeshift classroom with blackboard and chalk. I often played alone, upstairs in the unfinished attic, with my toys and created little future worlds out of nothing much. But the landscape is very real in my memory yet today. I could sense where I was headed, but unsure how to get there. However, in my mind I knew I would arrive if I really wanted it to happen.

There is a children's story called ***Roxaboxen*** by Alice McLerran and illustrated by Barbara Cooney that details a place that children made in Yuma, Arizona. It was said to be "a celebration of the active imagination, of the ability of children to create, even with the most unpromising materials, a world of fantasy so real and multidimensional that it earns a lasting place in memory." With the help of her mother's childhood manuscript, Alice McLerran was able to recreate this magical world from the stories the participants told and some written memories. The children constructed the makeshift town from stones, rocks, broken glass, desert plants and old, discarded junk. But to them it emerged as a play land that endures yet today in the memory of those children who created and inhabited it.

Think about it. Creative Vision is an active force in the development of who we are becoming. Our early years implant desires and outcomes into our subconscious minds and perhaps direct us to our future roles in life. Thinking back we move ahead to make real those play grounds that remain and give us our visions for today. A moment in time can point to our future careers as a predictor of our success and happiness. The only remaining question is, have we walked the path to our heart's desire or have we abandoned it for other more "secure" choices? Revisit your memories and decide for yourself. If you have made a wrong decision, there is still time to correct your course. Just do what brings you joy and satisfaction, and you will know when you have a strong foothold in where your spirit still wants to take you. As I look back to look to the future, I know that my dream is not finished. I have things yet to do, places to go, and tasks to accomplish since my role as educator is to help others achieve their dreams. My job is not finished until I see you working on your dream in building and inhabiting your own Roxaboxen! May it bring you the joy and happiness that you experienced as a child. Then, you will know that you have fully arrived.

++++++++++++++++++++++

Imagination: The Mirror of YOUR Soul
by Napoleon Hill

What a mighty power is *imagination,* the workshop of the soul, in which *thoughts* are woven into railroads and skyscrapers and mills and factories and all manner of material wealth.

> I hold it true that thoughts are things;
> They're endowed with bodies and breath and wings;
> And that we send them forth to fill
> The world with good results or ill.
> That which we call our secret thought
> Speeds forth to earth's remotest spot,
> Leaving its blessings or its woes,
> Like tracks behind it as it goes.
> We build our future, thoughts by thought,
> For good or ill, yet know it not,
> Yet so the universe was wrought.
> Thought is another name for fate;
> Choose, then, thy destiny and wait,
> For love brings love and hate brings hate.
> —Ella Wheeler Wilcox

If your *imagination* is the mirror of your soul, then you have a perfect right to stand before that mirror and see yourself as you wish to be. You have the right to see reflected in that magic mirror the mansion you intend to own, the factory you intend to manage, the bank of which you intend to be president, the station in life you intend to occupy. Your *imagination* belongs to you! Use it! The more you use it the more efficiently it will serve you.

Source: *Law of Success in Sixteen Lessons.* The Original Unedited Edition. Volume II. The Napoleon Hill Foundation. 2013. Pg. 70.

CHAPTER 42

If one advances confidently in the direction of his dreams, and endeavors to live the life which he has imagined he will meet with a success unexpected in common hours.
—HENRY DAVID THOREAU

Thoughts can be wild, wicked, and wonderful at the same time. You have heard the expression "in your wildest dreams," I am sure. People can put others down for their dreams of flight and fancy indicating that nothing EVER will come of them because they are just dreamers. In dreamland we can become whomever we care to be. King or pauper, a ranch hand or a bullfighter, a saint or a sinner, are all active players and real in our imaginary worlds. Oftentimes characters in fiction are more real to us than our next door neighbor. Who doesn't know Scrooge, Tom Sawyer, Heidi, Kermit and others who only first exist in the author's imagination? Who are your favorites in story and song? Are they real or figments of someone's imagination? Are you sure? It is easy to cross the line and speak of them as real in the sense of the material world, when in reality they are only the stuff that dreams are made of!

In a beautifully illustrated children's story entitled **Where The Wild Things Are,** author and illustrator Maurice Sendak creates a magical world of make believe for everyone to enjoy. Dressed in a wolf costume, little Max is sent to his room with no supper after acting out and getting into mischief. Pretending to be a wolf, he tells his mother "I'll eat you up!" With that statement, she had

reached her limit and put Max in time out. With time to think in his bedroom, Max imagines a place where wild things live and sails off to visit them. His trip takes over a year and when he reaches his destination, the Wild Things are tamed by his direct prolonged stare. Over time, Max cavorts with the beasts and has great fun as the King of the Wild Things. Soon, however, he is lonely and hungry and longs for home. He sails away, and the long voyage brings him right back to his safe bedroom where he finds his still hot supper waiting for him where Mom has left it.

This little boy's reverie is what can turn into future goals and actions. Max is able to travel mentally through his active imagination, and use creative vision in order to escape his bedroom timeout. It is a normal way to begin adult meditation and reflection in a world that the poet says is sometimes "too much with us." Interior, mental, visioning should be encouraged in the young as a ways and means to capture the wild ideas and things of interest that may or may not grow into our life's work. Through active imagination children can put themselves into a position of leadership and control that may not exist in their daily lives. Adults can use active imagination too in order to play out things in their minds that may lead to future performances or reconcile differences they are having in the world. If this technique works well and harms no one, why not use it? After all, adults are just grown up children.

Take the lead in your mental performance and see who you can envision yourself becoming today. It is just a short step into your future success as you see the "you" that you always knew you could be—wild thing that you are!

The Laws that Lead to Fortune
by Napoleon Hill

The earth on which you live, you, yourself, and every other material thing are the result of evolutionary change, through which microscopic bits of matter have been organized and arranged in an orderly fashion.

Moreover—and this statement is of stupendous importance—this earth, every one of the billions of individual cells of your body, and every atom of matter, *began as an intangible form of energy.*

Desire is thought impulse! Thought impulses are forms of energy. When you begin with the thought impulse, desire, to accumulate money, you are drafting into your service the same "stuff" that nature used in creating this earth, and every material form in the universe, including the body and brain in which the thought impulses function.

You can build a fortune through the aid of laws which are immutable. But, first, you must become familiar with these laws, and learn to use them. Through repetition, and by approaching the description of these principles from every conceivable angle, the author hopes to reveal to you the secret through which every great fortune has been accumulated. Strange and paradoxical as it may seem, the "secret" is not a secret. Nature herself advertises it in the earth on which we live, the stars, the planets suspended within our view, in the elements above and around us, in every blade of grass, and every form of life within our vision.

The principles which follow will open the way for understanding of imagination. Assimilate that which you understand, as you read this philosophy for the first time; then, when you reread and study it, you will discover that something has happened to clarify it, and give you a broader understanding of the whole. Above all, do not stop, nor hesitate in your study of these principles until you have read the book at least three times, for then, you will not want to stop.

Source: ***Think and Grow Rich.*** Ballantine Books. 1983. Pgs. 72-73.

PRINCIPLE 15

Maintenance of Sound Health

The mind and the body are so closely related that whatever one does affects the other. One does not enjoy sound health without a health consciousness. Sound health begins with a sound health consciousness, just as financial success begins with a prosperity consciousness. To maintain a health consciousness, one must think in terms of sound health, not in terms of illness and disease. As the old sayings go: "You have nothing if you do not have your health" and "If you think you're sick, you are."

CHAPTER 43

*In the face of uncertainty,
there is nothing wrong with hope.*
—BERNIE S. SIEGEL, M.D.

Maintenance of Sound Health takes on many shapes and forms throughout ours lives. It is not just physical health that we focus on daily, but rather emotional, spiritual, social, financial, and physical health all combine to contribute to our wellness or "dis"-ease. Sometimes it may be our bodily aches and pains that cause us concern, but on other days it may be a feeling of malaise that we cannot pinpoint or diagnose specifically that causes us to feel out of sorts or just simply down in the dumps. Usually, at those times, our concern is one of the other aspects of our being that is causing a pre-disposition to ill health that is more mental than physical.

Dr. Hill notes that people often suffer from hypochondria, and many people can even die from it! Hypochondria is an "imaginary" illness that can be very real to the patient. Worry, fear, dread, and lack of hope, cause many individuals to focus on an illness that they do not have, and predispose themselves to actually acquire it. Dr. Hill prescribes the cure for such illnesses as working daily to cultivate and maintain a positive mental attitude. Sad but true or glad but true, what we focus on we bring about in our lives. It is as simple and as profound as that.

Children too can be susceptible to these types of mental concerns. A children's story entitled ***Waiting for Benjamin: A***

Story about Autism deals with the feelings of an older brother whose younger sibling has autism. Often Alexander is angry, acts out, feels embarrassed and disappointed, and even neglected because his younger brother isn't like everyone else. Benjamin is different because he has been diagnosed with autism. Therefore, he gets special treatment due to his disability. This simple family configuration makes Alexander feel second class or excluded and also prevents him from feeling and behaving his best. He experiences anger due to the feeling of "it's not fair" that his brother gets all the extra attention and he does not.

The parents in this story recognize what is happening and attempt to explain to Alexander why Benjamin is the way he is. Mom and Dad also work with Alexander in order for him to feel more accepted and equally loved. As Alexander matures in understanding, he begins to hope that Benjamin will "catch up" in time and actually bond with him as a brother would. This story helps children express their feelings as to how they perceive what may or may not be happening. Once things are sorted out and explained, these misunderstandings that contribute to ill health, can be acknowledged and worked on toward a positive resolution.

Our mind-body powerhouse needs the fuel of PMA in order to operate properly. Without it, we can digress into types of symptoms that can lead to an unproductive life. These symptoms can be caught early and discussed so that children do not grow up with a negative mental attitude toward themselves and others. By learning about what is, each of us can do a better job at projecting what is yet to come. A future that is imagined with a positive mental attitude leads to a life that can become the same—positive in every way.

++++++++++++++++++++++

The Tremendous Powerhouse of Our Mind-Body
by Napoleon Hill

The proper perspective of this mind-body of ours is that the mind is the higher function of the two, and that the body is an exquisitely functioning machine for carrying the mind about and executing the dictates of this tremendous powerhouse. Yes, a smoothly functioning mind is necessary to a smoothly functioning body.

Think of those unfortunate individuals who have been bed-ridden, unable to do more than just talk or move a few fingers, who have lived full creative lives. This story can be multiplied and retold, with many names and places of those who refused to let crippled bodies stay them in their quest for greatness: Helen Keller, Pavlov, Nurmi the great runner, and Beethoven, to name a few.

The story of civilization is punctuated with greatness achieved by various individuals in spite of physical bankruptcy, because these individuals possessed smoothly functioning minds. Each of them has a *definite major purpose, faith* in that purpose and plan, and *faith* in *Infinite Intelligence*. They understood clearly where they were going and what their problem was.

Dr. Coyne Campbell, a well-know psychiatrist, said in one of his lectures on the problems of the maladjusted that they all had one problem in common. They were unable to tell him clearly what was the matter—they were unable to put their difficulties into words. He went on to say that when he had taught them to state their problem, they no longer needed his services. Once they had a clear picture of themselves and their problem and developed a *definite major purpose* and a *definite plan* to attain that purpose, these unfortunates were back on the road to a useful life.

The principles which follow will open the way for understanding of imagination. Assimilate that which you understand, as you read this philosophy for the first time; then, when you reread and study it, you will discover that something has happened to clarify it, and give you a broader understanding of the whole. Above all, do not stop, nor hesitate in your study of these principles until you have read the book at least three times, for then, you will not want to stop.

Individuals with weakened bodies like those mentioned earlier, seem always to have known their plan, or to have learned it at an early age. On the wings of a *definite major purpose, faith, enthusiasm,* and a *positive mental attitude,* they rose further and further from the vague despondency of maladjustment towards great heights of brilliance and achievement. This is the power of a man's mind. Thus it would seem that even when we cannot achieve sound physical health, we can achieve sound mental health if we have a *definite major purpose.*

Source: *PMA Science of Success.* Educational Edition. The Napoleon Hill Foundation. 1983. Pgs. 425-426.

CHAPTER 44

Optimism and humor are the grease and glue of life. Without both of them we would never have survived our captivity.
—PHILIP BUTLER, VIETNAM, POW

In health related matters, humor can heal. Just taking the time to see the humor inside the concern allows a person to shift perspective from worry to acceptance. When we size down the problem and look at it differently, we can oftentimes visualize different outcomes that may have eluded us. When we worry we devote too much time to potential problems. When we laugh, we massage our interior self and predispose ourselves to good solutions. Both are learned behaviors, but laughing is healthier than worrying.

There is a little Peanuts Wisdom book entitled **Me, Stressed Out?** that is fun to share with children. It includes snippets of wisdom concerning bad hair days, low test grades, the stress of baseball, things that couldn't get any worse, and life's biggest worries such as chocolate sundaes that drip down the side of the dish. Isn't it the truth that worries that start out as little inconsequential aggravations suddenly explode into worries that keep us awake at night?

We can stop worries in their tracks by taking ourselves less seriously. Worries infect our health, but only grow when fed. They gobble up our thoughts and quickly focus us on negative thinking. By guarding our mind's entryway, we can intentionally lock the door on worries and keep our distance and our healthy mental attitude. Worries can be evicted and told to never return. We are the landlord of our mind, and do not have to permit entry. Worries worry us and thereby produce more worries. They grow quicker that bamboo and soon invade the landscape of our minds.

By teaching ourselves and our children that we have a right to shut the door on worries, we take control of our thinking. Why not begin today to allow no thought that is negative to live in your mind space? You will find that once the door is closed and locked, you will have gained control of your thoughts. Permit no one to invade your thoughts. Show worry the door and only open it for preferred visitors that demonstrate a positive mental attitude. It can be said that you are known by the visitors you keep.

Prince of Sound Physical Health
by Napoleon Hill

The sole responsibility of this invisible guide is that of keeping my physical body in perfect order at all times, including the conditioning of the body for any adjustments which have to be made, such as that of preparation for dentistry. Before this Prince took over I was subject to headaches, constipation, and at times physical exhaustion, all of which have been corrected. The Prince of Sound Physical Health keeps all the vital organs of my body alert and functioning at all times, keeps the billions of individual cells of my body properly charged with bodily resistance, and *provides adequate immunity against all contagious diseases.*

Let it be remembered, however, that I cooperate with the Prince of Sound Physical Health by sensible living habits, such as proper eating, the right amount of sleep, *and habits which balance my work with an equal amount of play.* But particularly, I keep my mind occupied with positive, constructive thinking, and never permit it to engage in any form of fear, superstition or hypochondria. And lastly, with every morsel of food and every drop of liquid which goes into my mouth *I add a generous mixture of worship,* through which I express thanks to my invisible guide, the Prince of Sound Physical Health, for maintenance of perfect health throughout my body.

Source: *You Can Work Your Own Miracles.* Fawcett. 1971. Pgs. 48-49.

CHAPTER 45

*To every disadvantage there
is a corresponding advantage.*
—W. CLEMENT STONE

Life presents us with a series of changes that we must deal with over time. Like it or not, this is the cyclic nature of the universe and none of us are the exception, but rather the rule. Maintenance of Sound Health is a goal that should be foremost on our daily "to-do" list, but when we have our health we often take it for granted. Just like friendships, employment, spiritual practices, family, and close relationships, we fail to cultivate new beginnings and things once held dear deteriorate and fall by the wayside of life. Things we cherish are often not thought or cared about until they are gone. This is an aspect of human nature, but not one that we can take pride in since being in our "comfort zone" does little to motivate or inspire us to do more.

Life changes daily for children too, and these changes can move them into maturity quickly. A book written by Maria Shriver entitled **What's Happening To Grandpa?** deals realistically and lovingly with the topic of Alzheimer's Disease. As a family is confronted with Grandpa's memory loss, a young granddaughter  works on ways to help him remember and stay mentally close to the family. By creating a scrapbook with photos of Grandpa's life events, the granddaughter is able to hear Grandpa's stories as he relates them and to help him remember them for himself too. In a beautiful way, the cycle of life goes on. In anticipation of what is to come, the granddaughter honors Grandfather's life now and provides him with a testimonial to a life well lived and worthy of remembering.

By honoring our ancestors, we learn from them and begin to understand what sacrifices they made in our behalf. The cycle of ancestors, self, and descendants causes one to focus on the continuity of life. By helping children understand what has come before and what may come after, we are creating a bridge that will help them weather future storms and adversities as well as to celebrate life as it renews itself. This focus enables youngsters to envision a future that honors what was and is now and to bless it, as well as to anticipate what goodness they can contribute to what is yet to be.

✦✦✦✦✦✦✦✦✦✦✦✦✦✦✦✦✦✦✦✦✦✦

Ultimately, Nothing Matters
by Napoleon Hill

Nothing matters ultimately, so why fill you life with fear? Often I have noticed men and women who go through life afraid of this and afraid of that—as though they had tuned in on some cosmic wave-length which made fear an absolute virtue.

They had not tuned in, but rather had tuned out any influences beyond their own tiny affairs, which their own mind expanded to fill their cosmos. Fear is such a *little* thing!

Of course we go through life with "a decent respect for the opinions of mankind," as the Declaration of Independence says and now and then we defer to others and put their welfare ahead of our own. This is co-operation, not fear. It is civilization rather than anarchy. Yet look around and see how many people stretch their social consciences into consciences full of fear, depression and self-defeat. Why?—when ultimately, nothing matters? Do they think that if they slink through life instead of marching with head up, they will make their lives matter the more after they are dead? Marching through life with confidence and courage is a far more likely way to make yourself remembered; not a sure way, but far, far more likely. Again, if they are not concerned with the size of their tombstones, nor the flowers placed upon their graves, nor the prayers said in their memory—this is all the more reason for living fearlessly.

I once saw a book with the title *I Write As I Please.* I never was able to read the book, but I hope it lived up to its admirable title. Any man who dares to write as he pleases has gone a great distance toward finding peace of mind and holding it firmly.

This too I learned by trail and error. There was a time when an impressive corps of critics went over every line I wrote before my writings got into print. Then I began to see that I was being made to please the reader by pandering to his established prejudices and beliefs. What good would I do in that case?

Now I write as I please and let the chips fall where they may. Perhaps you have noticed this.

Source: *Grow Rich With Peace of Mind.* Ballantine Books Trade Edition. 1996.

PRINCIPLE 16

Budgeting Time and Money

People are divided into two classes: drifters and non-drifters. A non-drifter is a person who has a definite major purpose, a definite plan to attain that purpose, and is busily engaged in carrying out his plan. A drifter does no real thinking. He acts upon the thinking of others.

Successful people ask themselves the following questions:
- How are you using your time?
- How much of it are you wasting, and
- How are you wasting it?
- What are you doing to stop this waste?
- Tell me how you use your spare time and how you spend your money, and I will tell you where and what you will be ten years from now.

CHAPTER 46

*Every man is his own ancestor, and
every man his own heir. He devises his
own future, and he inherits his own past.*
—H. F. HEDGE

Almost every one of us are busy daily doing things that may not bring optimum results for the time that we invest in them. These things could be careless things, or thoughtless things, or daily things we do because of a routine that we have established. Probably the things that we do that hurt the most and those things that can and do affect another person negatively. Whether intentional or not, things that cause another person to suffer because of our carelessness, thoughtlessness, or just plain meanness are things that we need to correct first when budgeting our time and money.

Ask yourself if you always create a mess by leaving disorder wherever you go. Do dishes pile up, mail lay unopened, projects sit around half done, and people say, "I can tell that so-and-so has been here. Look at the mess!" If you see yourself in this picture perhaps you are just like the Busy Beaver who is always busy but fails to think things through. His actions always produce bad outcomes.

This little contemporary fable written and illustrated by Nicholas Oldland is entitled *The Busy Beaver*. Mr. Beaver is busy enough but he fails to think through his actions before they have an effect on Mr. Bear, Mr. Moose, and a family of homeless birds.

He rampages through the forest cutting down tree after tree with little concern as to what damage he is doing until one day a tree he fells falls in the wrong direction and pins him to the ground. He is hospitalized with many injuries. This time in recovery causes him to rethink his actions. He now sees that he has harmed himself and others too. While hospitalized, he decides to make amends to all whom he has injured with his overly enthusiastic approach to cutting down trees without a plan. First, he apologizes and next he uses his building skills to offer positive things to his "victims" in return for his carelessness. A flower pot for the bear's den, a canoe for the moose, and a new home for the family of birds.

The message is clear. Think things through before beginning any project. Don't only put yourself first, but consider others in your planning process. If you make a mistake, say "I'm sorry," and make true amends. And, when beginning anew, learn to budget your time and maintain a proper balance in all you do. It is said that leaving a "light footprint" upon the earth that does no harm to nature or others, is a good way to progress through life. Consider your own footprint as you trek through this life, and be gentle and kind to yourself and to all who follow after you. Because, what we leave behind is either our legacy or our curse for those who follow in our footsteps. Walk softly.

✦✦✦✦✦✦✦✦✦✦✦✦✦✦✦✦✦✦✦✦✦✦

Personal Inventory Time
by Napoleon Hill

This is your personal inventory time! You must find out *who you are, where you are going in life,* and *how you are going to get there.*

While looking for your best qualities we shall not overlook your worst qualities, for they must be removed before you can achieve the success and happiness you desire. For, if you are not where you want to be and what you wish to be, there is a definite reason. Let us find out what this reason is, and find out *now!*

If you do a good job of taking personal inventory, the chances are about a thousand to one, you will discover that you have been a *timewaster.* You are face to face with some facts which for the moment may not be pleasant. But, let us not pull any punches, but rather face these facts courageously.

Of course you have a good alibi with which to explain away your time-wasting habits. Everyone has! But alibis will not bring you what you desire of life.

Are you a success or a failure?

If you are a failure, no amount of explanation will change the results, for the one thing the world will never forgive is failure. The world wants successes; it worships successes; but it has no time for failures.

The only way a man can explain away his failure is by trimming his sails, through self-discipline, so that the later circumstances of his life will lead him to success. Success requires no alibis or explanations. Failure knocks alibis and explanations into a cocked hat. The world has decreed it to be thus.

It is a great day in a man's life when he sits down quietly and has a heart to heart talk with himself, for he is sure to make discoveries about himself which will be helpful, although his discoveries may give him a shock. Nothing is ever accomplished by wishing, hoping, or day-dreaming. Earnest self-analysis helps one to rise above these.

Source: ***PMA Science of Success.*** Educational Edition. The Napoleon Hill Foundation. 1983. Pgs. 459-460.

CHAPTER 47

*Come what may, time and the
hour runs through the roughest day.*
    —WILLIAM SHAKESPEARE

Time is a factor in our lives that most of us take for granted. The sayings, "all we have is time, we have all the time in the world, time waits for no man, time heals all wounds", and "time is money" all are in the common vernacular. Time is so common that it is often ignored and we assume that we have an unlimited supply. Like the air we breathe, we just assume it is there. Too often our time is spent in unworthy pursuits that advance us no further than we were before, and consequently our time is said to be wasted. Wasted time cannot be retrieved, but it can be mended in a fashion when we renew our commitment to spend our time wisely. Time that is focused allows us to forge a new path that leads us directly to our goal. We may think we want one thing and are really looking for another. We may never realize this fact until we are confronted with the outcome of the choices we have made in our lives.

In the children's book, **No Room for Napoleon,** we learn about the concept of sharing and enjoying the company of others. But, not a first. The dog Napoleon visits a small island seeking friendship and is invited to stay. He accepts, and soon he begins to overtake the island with his new home. Every rock and resource is put into his home using the free labor of his friends, Crab, Bunny, and Bear. When finished, the friends

decide their island is not the paradise that it once was and they sail away to another island nearby. Napoleon becomes lonely, and his kingdom is no place at all without his new friends. He leaves to seek them out. Worried that he will overtake their new home, his friends tell him that there is no more room for another member. Realizing that he was wrong to use all the resources for himself personally, Napoleon begs to stay because he is lonely. His friends relent, and under a new set of rules, Napoleon joins the group as an equal member, and not as their ruler. Napoleon learns too that it is important to respect both his friends and his shared environment.

When Napoleon's time was spent in getting and not giving, he neglected the rights of others. He did not see himself as selfish, but as privileged. He assumed that his friends were in agreement with him. But, the morning he woke up to find them gone, he realized life was lonely with only his status and glory to befriend him. His time was misspent, but he learned from his mistake and favored his friends over his possessions. When the group reunites, Napoleon realizes that the only person he should rule is himself, and the change that comes from within is better than any dictated change. The give and take of true friendship is a better standard to judge by, than by how much someone can do for you alone.

♦♦♦♦♦♦♦♦♦♦♦♦♦♦♦♦♦♦♦♦♦♦

My Commitment to Doctor Time
by Napoleon Hill

1. Time is my greatest asset, and I shall relate myself to it on a budget system which provides that every second not devoted to sleep shall be used for self-improvement.

2. In the future I shall regard the loss, through neglect, of any portion of my Time as a sin, for which I must atone by the better use in the future of an equivalent amount of it.

3. Recognizing that I shall reap that which I sow, I shall sow only the seeds of service which may benefit others as well as myself, and thereby throw myself in the way of the great Law of Compensation.

4. I shall so use my Time in the future that each day will bring me some measure of peace of mind, in the absence of which I shall recognize that the seed I have been sowing needs reexamination.

5. Knowing that my habits of thought become the patterns which attract all the circumstances affecting my life through the lapse of Time, I shall keep my mind so busy in connection with the circumstances I *desire* that no Time will be left to devote to fears and frustrations, and the things *I do not desire.*

6. Recognizing that, at best, my allotted Time on the earth plane is indefinite and limited, I shall endeavor in all ways possible to use my portion of it so that those nearest me will benefit by my influence, and be inspired by my example to make the best possible use of their own Time.

7. Finally, when my allotment of Time shall have expired, I hope I may leave behind me a monument to my name—not a monument in stone, but in the hearts of my fellowmen—a monument whose marking will testify that the world was made a little better because of my having passed this way.

8. I shall repeat this Commitment daily during the remainder of my allotment of Time, and back it with BELIEF that it will improve my character and inspire those whom I may influence, to likewise improve their lives.

Source: ***You Can Work Your Own Miracles.*** Napoleon Hill. Fawcett Gold Medal Books. New York. 1971. Pgs. 130-131.

CHAPTER 48

*It takes time to succeed because success is merely
the natural reward for taking time to do anything well.*
—JOSEPH ROSS

The concept of Time is an abstract one. Frequently, it is said that we all have the same 24 hours in a day, but most of us would agree that Time is not the same commodity for each and every one of us. Those of us with time on our hands wish away the minutes and the hours, and those of us with not enough time cannot gain another minute by wishing for one. Time is a commodity that is as elusive as quicksilver and most of us cannot put our finger on exactly why it speeds up or slows down against our best plans and wishes.

It has been stated that how we respect time determines how opportunity respects us. As we unravel this statement, it appears to mean that the amount of quality time we invest in our desire, passion, or definite major purpose is in correlation with how we encounter opportunities that work in our behalf. What we think about we attract, and what we spend time on we draw into our physical world. We know that time waits for no man, but the time we devote to self-discipline in completing the task before us eventually brings us results that are more often than not positive. W. Clement Stone's manta "Do It Now" works because we devote the time to work it. Stated another way, what we invest time in during the day delivers results proportionate to the dedicated time, effort, and self-discipline that we put into it.

There are many time management systems, but for me a simple goal sheet or daily "to do" it sheet listing ten or fewer priority items works best. In the morning, I ask myself what it is I would like to accomplish today, and then I write it down. Usually, I take great pride in crossing major items off my list. I have invested Time in accomplishing these items and when they are completed they are crossed off, not erased! It brings closure to the item and also allows me to move on to my next goal.

A fun children's story entitled *What Time Is It, Mr. Crocodile?* by Judy Sierra and illustrated by Doug Cushman, develops over the concept of a "to do" list gone awry due to five pesky monkeys that invade Mr. Crocodile's day. The list of things to do cannot be done because the monkeys continually tease him and distract him. The monkeys he planned to catch for food, turn the tables on Mr. Crocodile and befriend him. Exhausted, he states: "Time to say, 'I was rude, with a bad attitude, and I'd much rather have you as friends than as food.'" He now reads to them, shops with them, cooks with them and sings to them. His modified "to do" list includes rather than excludes his new friends, and surprisingly he is the happier for it.

We all need to be reminded that Time needs to be shared with others in teamwork and mastermind alliances in order to make the most of our Time. We can expand our time with the engagement of others just as leaders expand their presence with the aid of those people who support their mission or purpose in life. By engaging rather than disconnecting from the playful monkeys that pester us, we learn to achieve compounded time that can work to everyone's advantage. By mastering time, we can attain our goal. By engaging others in our timely pursuits, we can create a destiny, even leave a legacy, that will endure beyond time.

++++++++++++++++++++++++

How Your Time Should Be Budgeted
by Napoleon Hill

Effectiveness in human endeavor calls for the organized budgeting of time. And experience, both that of successful men and those who have failed, has proved that no one may be sure of personal success without a careful time budgeting system. For the average man the twenty-four hours of the day should be divided as follows:

a. Eight hours for sleep.
b. Eight hours for work in connection with your occupation.
c. Eight hours for recreation and spare time activities.

There are few circumstances under which anyone may take liberties with the first eight hour period which belongs to sleep, for nature has set aside this portion of one's time for rest and the rebuilding and repair of the physical body, and for other bodily functions which require complete relaxation.

The second eight hours represent the period which experience has proved to be necessary for work in connection with your business, trade or profession. Here you have a wide range of choices as to the use you make of your time. You may use it so that it will yield nothing. Or you may use it so that it will bring only the bare necessities of life. Or you may use it so that it will bring you all the riches that your life demands or requires. The use made of this time will depend partly, if not entirely, upon whether you are a drifter or a person with a *definite major purpose*.

> *The happiest men are those who have learned to mix play with their work and bind the two together with enthusiasm.*

The third eight hour period, known as spare time, holds the secret of all great achievement. It is the *balance of power* which may be thrown into any type of endeavor you desire.

This is the period which enables you to follow the habit of *going the extra mile,* a habit which is, and always will be, an essential for success in the higher brackets of human endeavor.

Successful men recognize the value of spare time, and they agree that it can be made the most profitable of the three periods of the day. Necessity forces one to devote the first eight hour period to sleep and the second eight hour period to work. But the third period belongs to each individual—to you—to use as you choose.

Successful men have been wise enough to organize and use their spare time so that it will serve both the purpose of recreation and the development of future opportunities. They have found recreation of the highest order in the constructive use of *creative vision,* planning ways and means of promoting themselves into higher and better stations in life, making new friends, experimenting with their most cherished ideas, and helping others to find their places in life.

Source: *PMA Science of Success.* Educational Edition. The Napoleon Hill Foundation. 1983. Pgs. 481-482.

PRINCIPLE 17

Cosmic Habitforce

Cosmic Habitforce pertains to the universe as a whole and the laws that govern it. Cosmic Habitforce is Infinite Intelligence in operation. It is a sense of order. It takes over a habit and causes a person to act upon the habit automatically. Developing and establishing positive habits leads to peace of mind, health, and financial security. You are where you are and what you are because of your established habits and thoughts and deeds.

CHAPTER 49

Ask not that events should happen as you will, but let your will be that events should happen as they do, and you shall have peace.
—EPICTETUS

Young or old, it doesn't matter. We all spend time wondering about the significance of our existence. Where did we come from? Why are we here? And, where are we going? These life questions perplex many of us, yet the proposed answers are only guesses as to the real meaning of the Universe and its intentions regarding each of us. Dr. Hill defines this principle of life as Cosmic Habitforce and labels it justly the Comptroller of the Universe. He indicates that when we work in unison with Nature, our outcomes move in tandem with the Universal Force. Simply put, this means acknowledging that we are part of Nature and all its wonderment and not separate from it. We are in creation and creation is within us. This mystery can be stated simply in a few words, yet the profundity of it all continues to elude our comprehension since none of us knows the mind of the Creator. Just by believing, holding on to faith, and having hope for the most positive outcome, is the best that can be utilized by us in this lifetime. The rest remains mystery.

Children come into life with simple understandings of the process. As they mature, naturally they ask more questions regarding their reason for being. A child's storybook written by Chara M. Curtis and illustrated by Cynthia Aldrich entitled ***All I See Is Part Of Me*** introduces the child to his position and part in the Universe. This book wonderfully introduces children to the concept of wholeness within the system of Creation. It explains the concept that each of us is and remains a part of everything we see and experience and also everything is a part of each of us. The concept of "star child" is woven into these few pages and causes the reader to pause and reflect on the nature of Creation and our part in the process.

Cosmic Habitforce literally puts us in our place and causes each of us to consider what our contribution to life may be. By being a contributor and not only a consumer, we can co-create what is to come next. By understanding what is often termed the "Golden Rule" we arrive at the realization that what we do to ourselves we also do to others and most importantly we are the 'others' too. This synchronicity compels us to consider our synergistic part in the unity of all things. In the children's book the child asks: "Sister Star, how can it be/That I am you and you are me?" The star glows and responds: "You're larger than you know,/You are everyplace there is to go. You have a body, this is true. . ./But look at what's inside of you!"

Energy is neither created or destroyed and therefore the saying "what goes around comes around" is technically true. At one time or another, we could have been or yet become the fragrance in the honeysuckle, the purr in the kitten, the ray of starlight, or the taste of pumpkin pie. Uniquely, however, we are spiritual beings having a physical experience in the here and now. How lucky for us that we can and are part and parcel to the system of the Universe that so lovingly included us in the creation of all that is. Let your little light shine while becoming the shinning star you are akin to as well.

The child in the children's book responds to the star as he states: "Thank you so much, Sister Star! I love the part of me you are." If we learn the lesson of Cosmic Habitforce, we too can embrace the Universe and benefit from the interaction too. Within and without we are the starlight that can illuminate the world.

The Creator Whom I Know
by Napoleon Hill

The Creator whom I know is not separated from me by light-years nor by any other distance. I see evidence of His existence in every blade of grass, every flower, every tree, every creature on this earth, in the order of the stars and the plants which float out there in space, in the electrons and protons of matter, and most especially in the marvelous working principles of the human mind and the body within which it operates.

If you would rather speak of a force or a presence for a limitless intelligence rather than a Creator, it is the same. It is there. Is it affected by our worship? I doubt it. Can we sometimes attune ourselves so that we receive help from universal vibrations? This, I believe, is almost certainly true.

I do not even attempt to guess the over-all purpose or plan behind the universe. So far as I can tell, there is not a plan for man except to come into this world, live a little while, and go. While he lives he is given the opportunity to make himself and his fellow men better beings, perhaps a more advanced form of man, as Lecomte du Noüy suggests. But—his ultimate purpose? I do not think anyone knows more about that than I know, and I know nothing about it.

Source: *Grow Rich! With Peace of Mind.* Ballantine Books. New York. 1996. Pgs. 231-232.

CHAPTER 50

The light of God surrounds me,
The love of God enfolds me,
The power of God protects me,
The Presence of God watches over me,
Wherever I am, God is.
—PRAYER CARD

Old Turtle is a story by Douglas Wood with watercolors by Cheng-Kee Chee. Dealing with ecology, peace, and the interconnectedness of all things in the Universe, it uses an old, wise turtle to propose the answers to existence. At first all things in creation see the Creator as having characteristics connected to their worldview. For example, the stone  defines the Creator as a great rock that never moves. The breeze disagrees and says that the Creator is a wind who is never still. Next, the mountain chimes in stating that the Creator is a snowy peak, high above the clouds. At first softly, and then loudly the disagreement develops and becomes an argument among all creation that causes the Old Turtle to speak up. After crediting each idea as true, she goes on to add that God is all that and more.

The turtle knowingly states: "God is gentle and powerful. Above all things and within all things. God is all that we dream of, and all that we seek, all that we come from and all that we can find. God IS." And, the turtle adds, "There will soon be a new family of beings in the world, and they will be strange and wonderful. They will be reminders of all that God is."

And the people came, and they are us. All shapes, all colors, all languages, and with the ability to have their thoughts soar beyond the earth, they will have the capacity to cherish the earth and its creatures, but they too soon forgot their mission. Instead they hurt the earth. But next, like a miracle, the creatures of the earth intervene by acknowledging that now the mountain can see God in the sea, the ocean can see God in the mountain peaks, and the breeze can see God in the rocks, and they realize that the Old Turtle's lesson is true. God is in everything and everywhere. What happens next is ever more miraculous. The world's people began to listen and to see God in one another and also in the earth's marvelous beauty, but it took a very long time. But it does happen. And, at the end the Old Turtle smiles, and so does God.

The fable is a profound one. Today, we are at a very scary juncture in the history of the earth. People are alienated, lonesome, tired, and forlorn because they do not see earth's interconnectedness in all things and are inhumane to each other and take for granted God's gifts. Man's inhumanity to man and to all that is, prevents the world from being a better place in which to live. Lacking the Golden Rule and pursuing the rule of gold, man defiles all the gifts given to him at birth by the Creator. Until the switch in thinking occurs to embrace rather than to exclude everyone and everything in creation, the earth will become a place of torment rather than beauty. The only salvation is to hear the Old Turtle's message and to begin again from a new perspective that embraces all that is for the good of all humanity by practicing the rule given to us from the beginning—treat others as we would like to be treated ourselves. That is the process, simple and complete, to making the world a better place in which to live and it begins and ends with each one of us.

++++++++++++++++++++++

The Great Miracle of Life
by Napoleon Hill

The stars and planets, and the nebulous matter from which these were formed, are related to one another by nature's habits of fixation, operating through the Law of Cosmic Habitforce. Day and night, the seasons of the year, the law of balance, and every living thing except man, are bound by inexorable habits which make their movements and actions accurately predictable over long periods of time and far in advance of the happenings.

Man alone has been given the privilege of fixing his own earthly destiny, with the right to make it pleasant or unpleasant, successful, or unsuccessful, happy or unhappy, rich or poor, and his achievements are always unpredictable because his potential power is unlimited.

If man had but two more privileges than he now possesses he would be on an equal footing with the Creator; namely (1) the privilege of coming into the world at birth, of his own choice; and (2) the privilege of remaining among the living as long as he desires. Man has potential control over almost everything else, but alas, he rarely discovers the powers available to him or makes any attempt to use these powers for his own uplift, or to make this a better world.

For the most part, man settles down in a sort of tug-of-war struggle with forces which become unfriendly toward him because he does not understand them—forces such as the great miracles of life—and he gladly settles with life for a place to sleep, a little food to fill his belly and enough clothes to hide his nakedness.

Source: *You Can Work Your Own Miracles.* Fawcett Gold Medal Books. New York. 1971. Pg. 120.

CHAPTER 51

I thank You God for this most amazing day;
for the leaping greenly spirits of trees and a
blue true dream of sky; and for everything
which is natural which is infinite which is yes.
—E.E. CUMMINGS

Children are our future. The legacy that we leave and create is for them. They alone will walk the planet Earth and maybe beyond because of the footsteps we have taken. Whether they recede or advance is a consequence of what we have left behind during our own journey. If something is good and holy and we fail to pass on the significance of what we treasure, whose fault is it? If the Earth could talk, much wisdom would be heard for those capable of listening. For others, it is our duty to share the knowledge that we have accumulated and to pass it on. Otherwise, it is lost to the ages.

In teaching Napoleon Hill's Philosophy of Success, I sense a gap within our outreach to the younger generation. It is the purpose of these essays to bridge that gap with children's stories that mirror the teachings of Dr. Hill. The themes from the children's stories can open the door to a developing interest in Dr. Hill's teachings as children grow up. In this manner, we can begin to lay a new foundation for those youngsters advancing to study and internalize the interests, opinions, ideas, values, and beliefs that Dr. Hill espouses as the keys to success for individuals and ultimately the world.

A children's story, entitled *Sofia's Dream,* is written by Land Wilson and illustrated by Sue Cornelison. It shares Sofia's love for and conversation with the Moon. One night, Sofia witnesses the Moon in its blue phase and wants to understand why the Moon is sad. The Moon invites Sofia to visit during her dreams in order to understand what the Moon is experiencing, and she does. In her visit, she sees the Earth from the Moon's perspective and is saddened too. The Moon states, "Your Mother Earth is  where you live. / She is my closest relative, / Also home for nature's wonder, / Now she's saddened by real plunder." The Moon adds, "Her people seem so unaware, / That what Earth needs is better care."

Sofia is told that she must learn about what she and others can do to protect and care for the Earth. In the scheme of things, everything makes a difference, and Sofia realizes that she can help by aiming high herself, and also inspire others to do the same. She realizes that "Once you see from this distant view, / Awareness may come over you. / By far your gift of greatest worth, / Is our dear home, this planet Earth."

Our actions either make our Earth a heaven or a hell by how we treat it. We choose the metaphor now, and it will surely play out in the lives of the children of the world in the future. Why not envision a heaven on Earth and work to make it so? "What the mind can conceive and believe, the mind can achieve!" But it takes action too to create the outcome. Won't you join us in the worthy quest? I hope so.

✦✦✦✦✦✦✦✦✦✦✦✦✦✦✦✦✦✦✦✦✦✦

The Power of the First Cause
by Napoleon Hill

This much the author does know—that there is a power, or a First Cause, or an Intelligence, which permeates every atom of matter, and embraces every unit of energy perceptible to man—that this Infinite Intelligence converts acorns into oak trees, causes water to flow down hill in response to the law of gravity, follows night with day, and winter with summer, each maintaining its proper place and relationship to the other. This Intelligence may, through the principles of this philosophy, be induced to aid in transmuting desires into concrete, or material form. The author has this knowledge, because he has experimented with it—and has experienced it.

Source: *Think and Grow Rich.* Ballantine Books. New York. 1983. Pg. 194.

CHAPTER 52

North Pole—December 2015

Dear Friends of Napoleon Hill:

I hope this message finds you well and blessed with the joy of the holiday season. What an extraordinary year this has been for the inspiration and wonder seen right here in the work being done at the Napoleon Hill World Learning Center. For me it has made the task of Christmas gifting this year so easy. Every child on my list, naughty or nice, is receiving a book come Christmas morning.

For those of you who desire to introduce the principles of success to children, and I hope it's many of you, this book introduces 52 children's books with a relevant message consistent with the teachings of Napoleon Hill. What a brilliant way to open the minds of people of all ages and reinforce the value of reading books. An art form that remains precious in this world of technology, books provide such inspiration and wonder. The chapter by chapter descriptions of each children's book, woven together with one of Dr. Hill's 17 Principles, was written with such enlightenment and generosity by Judith Williamson, Director of the Napoleon Hill World Learning Center.

One of my favorite entries is the book **What Do You Do With An Idea?** written by Kobi Yamada and illustrated by Mae Besom. As Judy notes, "It inspires and explains what you do with an idea. In allowing it to grow and giving it the environment that it needs to transform itself into something special, you 'gift' your idea to the world. By setting an idea free you learn that it can now be part of everything for everyone. It parallels Dr. Hill's mantra of 'Conceive it, Believe it, Achieve it.' One idea at a time, freed up, can indeed change the world."

How marvelous! My sleigh is filled with copies of ***Putting the Principles Into Practice*** so that children around the world can be inspired and begin to learn the values and beliefs taught by Dr. Napoleon Hill and brought to life in the 52 chapters that Judy Williamson has authored. And, as a bonus, two certified instructors of The Napoleon Hill Foundation, Havilah Malone and Diane Lampe, have authored 17 corresponding stories to bring the principles alive right now for children this Christmas. These are included with beautiful illustrations done by Youjin Oh, another student of Dr. Hill from South Korea. What a blessing to have these three women share their talent with youngsters around the world. Santa will have to make certain that there is something extra in their Christmas stockings this year too!

The holiday season and the reflection of another year gone by is a time for recognizing the power of Cosmic Habitforce, which as Napoleon Hill writes, "pertains to the universe as a whole and the laws that govern it. It is a sense of order. You are where you are and what you are because of your established habits and thoughts and deeds...The major distinguishing characteristic of Cosmic Habitforce is that it forces all repeated actions to become fixed habits... ."

I encourage all of you as you look forward to the New Year, to make reading books a repeated action and a fixed habit. Read books for yourself. Read books to your young children. And make sure your older children are reading books. And why not give a book as a gift this holiday season instead of one more technological device? You have quite the list to choose from in Judy's collection.

I can't duplicate Judy's talent for writing (making toys and flying a sleigh is my thing, you remember), but I wanted to share in this space what has always been my favorite children's book, "Winnie the Pooh."

"A Bear of Very Little Brain," as author A.A. Milne refers to Pooh time and time again, we see through his adventures that Pooh is anything but of very little brain. It was, after all, the *Brain of Pooh* that saved dear Piglet from the Very Great Danger during The Terrible Flood. In his timeless classic from 1926, Milne and his brilliant illustrator, Ernest H. Shephard, show how Pooh, along with his charming friends from the Hundred Acre Wood, face trials and tribulations with most all of Dr. Hill's 17 Principles and especially the guidance of Cosmic Habitforce.

"When you wake up in the morning, Pooh," says Piglet, "what's the first thing you say to yourself?"

"What's for breakfast," said Pooh. "What do you say, Piglet?"

"I say, I wonder what's going to happen exciting today?" said Piglet.

Pooh nodded thoughtfully.

"It's the same thing," he said.

In the New Year ahead, may your mornings be filled with healthy and hearty breakfasts, your days filled with joy and exciting things and if they are the same thing—like a rich pot of honey—so much the better!

Merry Christmas and a Happy New Year!
Santa Claus

All the Best to You,

Napoleon Hill

THE NAPOLEON HILL FOUNDATION

presents

The Amazing Adventures of Oliver Hill

by
Havilah Malone and Diane Lampe

17 Short Stories based on
The Principles of Success
by *Think and Grow Rich*
Author, Napoleon Hill

About the Authors

Prior to becoming certified, each leader certification candidate is required to complete a project related to the 17 Success Principles that are the basis of the curriculum for certification. The project must be done voluntarily as a "give-back" to the Foundation without compensation. Diane and Havilah's combined project is the treasury of children's rhymed stories that incorporate the 17 Success Principles as an introduction to the Science of Success for early readers.

Havilah Malone is an Author and Speaker from New Orleans who graduated from college at the age of nineteen with a degree in Arts & Communications and a minor in Psychology. Havilah is also a youth advocate and founder of the non-profit foundation *Living Beyond the Box, Inc.* The foundation's premiere program, *Everybody Loves Barbie,* fosters a self-empowerment movement that helps youth break the silence of abuse and develop the courage and confidence to live life on their own terms. Havilah is the youngest of four brothers and sisters and attributes much of her success to the Napoleon Hill principles she learned as a youth. She is a Certified Instructor for the Napoleon Hill Foundation.

Diane Lampe is President and COO of The Lampe Company, LLC, a financial services business she owns and operates with her husband, Bill. Diane has used Napoleon Hill's master work, *The Law of Success,* in building the business for the past 10 years. She attributes much of their success to understanding and teaching Napoleon Hill's 17 Principles of Success. As a mother and recent grandmother, she has spent years in raising their children to believe that the path to success is through applying these success principles. Now, she is working toward taking Hill's principles to the next generation. She is a Certified Instructor for the Napoleon Hill Foundation.

Introduction

*Whatever the mind can conceive
and believe, the mind can achieve.*
—NAPOLEON HILL

Welcome to an Amazing Adventure you will not soon forget
of Oliver, Olivia, and Big Zeke who you've not yet met.
You'll also meet their friends, who are very much like you,
enjoying life and every day learning something new.
These lessons from Dr. Hill will guide you your whole life through
into a wonderful world of possibilities that you never knew.
As you read these amazing adventures keep an open mind,
deep inside lie hidden treasures that you are sure to find.
Let the journey begin as you Make Your Dreams Come True.

All the Best,
Happy Wishes to You!
Havilah & Diane

THE AMAZING LEMONADE STAND
#1 Definiteness of Purpose

It was another sunny day,
and Oliver was dreaming away.
How could he get his brother and sister
to come out and play?

Olivia was always busy
laughing with her friends.
In her own small world playing pretend.

His older brother Big Zeke
had his head stuck in a book.
Oliver pleaded, "Look, Big Zeke look...
those books can wait another day.
Please come out and play!"

Big Zeke shook his head, "not today,"
and Olivia just laughed him away.

Oliver with head hanging low for all to see,
went and sat by his favorite lemon tree.
Deciding that he would find a way
to get Big Zeke and Olivia to come out and play!

His little puppy Cody mischievous as could be,
grabbed a lemon from the lemon tree.

He brought it to Oliver, but wouldn't let it go.
Oliver stood up and shouted, "Now I know!
A lemonade stand is what it will be

for Big Zeke, Olivia, and me!"

With Mom and Dad's help, work was under way
and Oliver's excitement and giggling
could be heard throughout the day.

Big Zeke began to peek from behind his book,
and Olivia's curiosity brought her outside to look.

Neither could believe what they saw with their eyes,
the amazing family lemonade stand. What a big surprise!

Big Zeke and Olivia asked Oliver,
"Can we come over and play?"
"Of course," Oliver replied,
"that would make my day!"

Oliver was so excited
that his dream had come true
of getting his big brother and sister
to play with him as he knew he could do.

THE ICE CREAM CONTEST
#2 Mastermind Alliance

It was that special time of year,
when the county fair hit high gear.
People came from everywhere
to compete in contests at the fair.

Oliver wanted to find something
    he could do
to participate in the contests too.
When he looked down the list to
    his surprise,
an ice cream flavor contest caught his eye.

He thought what a fun contest that would be,
to create a yummy flavor and win easily.
And getting to eat ice cream all day
wasn't such a bad price to pay.

The milk from his cow was of the highest grade
and would create the best ice cream ever made.

He knew he couldn't do it alone
so he decided to pick up the phone.
Oliver thought to himself, "Who will I call
that can make a flavor that would be pleasing to all?"

"Julie, Julie that's who,
she makes the best sweets. I love them. Don't you?"
He asked Julie to come and she readily agreed,
"A new ice cream flavor, that's brilliant indeed!"

"Wait there's more," Oliver chimed in,
"we still need a helping hand to ensure our win.
Who came to mind, well wouldn't you know...
It was our friend and good neighbor, Joe!"

He had the strength to churn ice cream all day.
Just add sugar and cream and the best milk in town,
and with Julie's flavor they'll win best all around.

The work began and the fun did too,
eating lots of ice cream was a dream come true.
When the flavor hit their tummies, everyone agreed
it would be the winner guaranteed.
Now came the day the country fair had arrived.
"We were ready. Julie, Joe, and I."

"As the judges tasted all the flavors that were there,
we were right, our ice cream was beyond compare.
We won the trophy and took first prize,
doing it together, Julie, Joe, and I."

THE BIGGEST SPLASH
#3 Applied Faith

Another summer was to come and pass
without Oliver experiencing a splash.
Since no one ever taught him how to swim,
his fear grew bigger and bigger and overcame him.

He watched all his friends and it made him sore,
as they jumped in and splashed and made quite a roar.
His secret desire was to learn how to swim,
but he was afraid his friends would make fun of him.

It was the hottest day of the year
and again Oliver was full of fear.
He avoided the water the best he could,
but no one really understood.

His teacher Mrs. Judy saw the
    fright on his face.
She was confused, that look was
    so out of place.
"Oliver, my dear, tell me what's wrong?"

Ashamed and embarrassed, Oliver quietly said,
"I don't know how to swim, so I stand here instead.
My friends will laugh because I don't,
so I never tried, and I won't."

With a warm smile Mrs. Judy lovingly said,
"You can do it if you believe you can.
I will teach you, just take my hand."

Mrs. Judy began giving lessons to him.
He learned how to float,
even backstroke and swim.

Oliver's confidence grew very strong
because he took action to move it along.

Summer was leaving with haste
and there was no time to waste.

Oliver ran to the great swimming hole
to finally accomplish a lifelong goal.
Jumping right in for the biggest splash of the year,
once and for all getting rid of his fear!

MEATLOAF MONDAY
#4 Going the Extra Mile

Monday is this family's favorite day of the week.
Ready to eat, the kids head off to seek
the delicious food prepared by their Mother.
She makes a mean meatloaf like no other.

What sets it apart from all of the rest
are the freshest ingredients that have passed the test.

Each of the children has a part to play
in gathering fresh farm food for Meatloaf Monday.

The journey begins to find the best of the best
as Big Zeke, Olivia and Oliver set out for the quest.

As they approach the tall tomato vine,
Big Zeke grabbed a ladder and started to climb.
Olivia said, "not that one, go to the top,
only the juiciest from this crop."

Now that Big Zeke's sack is full off they all go
to find the next ingredient in Mom's meatloaf.

Oliver said, "Let's protect our eyes,
because strong onions can make you cry."
So out came the goggles from Oliver's sack,
Big Zeke and Olivia were happy he made the pack.

With a pep in their step and singing a song,
they went down each row and gathered along,
not the bruised ones or brown ones or ones with holes,
only firm onions in their sacks could meet their goals.

Even though the kids' tummies began to growl
it would not stop them from going the extra mile.

As they passed the garlic, Olivia grabbed a couple of cloves,
now to the chicken coop they had to go past the groves.

Yippee, one more ingredient to place in their sacks
was the farm fresh eggs so they would not crack.

Now that their quest is finally complete,
They pick up their sacks and head home to eat.

Mom and Dad met them at the door with a smile,
"We're proud of you for going the extra mile."

When the family sat down to eat,
all agreed this was the Meatloaf Monday to beat!
It was far superior than all of the rest.
This Meatloaf Monday more than passed the test.

YOU MAKE ME SMILE
#5 Pleasing Personality

When Olivia walks into a room
    with a big smile on her face,
her energy is felt all over
    the place.

Olivia shines a light wherever
    she goes.
Her light comes from inside,
    everyone knows.

To this fact, her teachers
    can attest
Olivia always tries to do her very best.

She's cooperative and respectful
    and strives for success.
And works really hard to do well on
    her tests.

Olivia may struggle a time or two
learning something new as most
    people do
but she'll find a way to see it through.

Even when change isn't easy to embrace,
she keeps a positive expression on her face.

As she gets on the bus at the end of the day,
Olivia sees her brother who had nothing to say.

He was looking out the window at a sky so grey.
Feeling sad and alone, wanting it to go away.

She sits next to him wearing a big grin,
"Oliver, whatever it is will go away,
I'm here for you if you want me to stay."

Oliver quickly replied, "Of course I do,
I already feel better because of you."

Olivia then shared, "Whenever I feel down
a big smile always helps to turn it around.
I instantly feel better inside and out,
when a kind word is spoken when I'm in doubt."

Olivia's big smile makes people feel good.
She has a big smile as everyone should.

CAMP FIRE FUN
#6 Personal Initiative

The packing and planning was done,
now the boys were headed to Camp
    Fire Fun.

Camp Counselor Brown said with
    delight,
"To make this trip easy from the start,
each of us must play our part."

"How good you do is up to you,
we'll see how well you follow through.
Here's your assignments so gather round,
no cutting corners or trashing camp ground."

"Neil and Will – gather wood and make a big pile,
the bigger the pile the bigger my smile."

As the rest of the assignments were handed out,
all of the boys began to shout,
"We're so happy we are going to see a bear,
roast marshmallows and tell stories that scare."

Off into the woods the boys began to go.
When Neil and Will came back wouldn't you know...
Neil's wood pile was so very low.

He only brought back four pieces
no, it was three...
a pile so low, as low as could be.

Next came Will, who always went the extra mile
and what do you know, he had a really big pile!

He brought back not eight...not even nine,
but came back to camp with twenty-four in a line.

Neil cornered Will and sarcastically said,
"Why did you bring back that much wood,
it makes it look like I did less than I should?"

Will replied with confidence in his voice,
"I did it because it was the right choice.
We'll have a big fire when all the work is done.
You should try it; you'll have so much more fun."

Neil thought about why he didn't try harder,
just trying to get by shows he's not a self-starter.
He wanted to change and change he would,
by doing it again the very best he could.

Into the woods Neil went at a quick pace,
with a new found attitude seen on his face.
He brought back such a humongous pile
that Camp Counselor Brown had to smile.

In the dark of night the fire blazed bright
and all the boys cheered in sheer delight.
They agreed this trip was #1,
truly unforgettable Camp Fire Fun!

OLIVIA'S NEW BIKE
#7 Positive Mental Attitude

One of the best events of the year
is the school bike race that was drawing
 near.

Olivia wanted to enter the race
so she could win and take first place.

The problem was she didn't have a bike
or the money to buy one that she
 would like.

So she decided to ask her mom for the money.
Her mom replied, "Sorry, we don't have it, Honey."

"There's a bike in the garage, covered with dust
you know the one...that is all full of rust?
It needs new parts and a little work too,
but that could be the solution for you."

Olivia excitedly said, "Mom, what a wonderful idea!
With my brothers' help, we could find the right parts.
There's no way I could lose...I'm ready to start!"

Her brothers agreed and off they all went,
looking for parts that wouldn't cost a cent.

They gathered two tires, brakes and pedals,
shiny used parts that were all full of metal.
They found handle bars and a comfy seat too

and a strong chain link that looked brand new.

Olivia was overjoyed they found what they needed.
In their search for the right parts they truly succeeded.

Today the school race was finally here.
Friends and family were lined up to cheer.

In the beginning Olivia took off at a very fast pace,
but she never practiced and was all over the place.

After crossing the finish line she jumped up and down.
Although everyone was surely expecting a frown.

With a confused look on the crowd's face,
her brothers blurted out, "You didn't win the race!"

With a beaming smile Olivia cheerfully replied,
"I know I didn't win but I still had so much fun
even without winning I still feel like number one.
Spending time together building this bike with you
was so much better than buying one brand new."

"Now I can practice and prepare for the race,
with your help next year I will take first place!"

THE TOWN OF LOST AND FOUND
#8 Enthusiasm

Fear and famine filled the *Town of Lost and Found,*
wherever you looked no food was around.

The farmer's son Oliver saw his mother in tears.
He wanted to fix it and get rid of her fears.

Remembering his grandfather's story
about a seed that grows when fed,
not with water but *LOVE* instead.

He dug out the seeds from a secret
   chest.
Excited and ready to save his town,
Oliver ran screaming and shouting,
"Look what I found!"

The people scoffed and laughed
and shooed him away.

The young man Oliver decided,
I'll Do It Anyway!
"If It's To Be, It's Up To Me,"
said Oliver enthusiastically.

In a hurry he ran home as fast as he could,
knowing that he could do so much good.

Holding each seed in his hand, eyes closed tight,
he sang this song with all his might,

*"Oh seed, oh seed I am grateful to thee,
I give you all the love I have within me."*

That night as he laid his head upon his bed,
his burning desire was for his town to be fed.

By morning the seeds started to sprout.
As the postman passed by he began to shout,
"Look, I can't believe they are really out!"

Oliver exclaimed,
"More love, more love is what we need
to make them grow faster indeed."

The postman then spread the word from house to house,
"The more love you give, the more the seeds will sprout."

Oliver went on to save the town...
they were no longer lost but finally found.

THE BIG SPELLING BEE
#9 Self-Discipline

Whenever you see Big Zeke
you'll only catch a glimpse of his eyes.
His head will be in a book,
to his friends that's no surprise.

Last week he brought home a trophy
for winning the Big Spelling Bee.
This was no small feat, as you will soon see.

At school, Mr. Martinez had news to share
and his excitement was without compare.

"We are going to the Regional Spelling Bee.
Big Zeke you are the one chosen to compete."

With a stunned and terrified look in his eyes,
Big Zeke found this news a very big surprise!

Mr. Martinez continued...
"We know you'll be the one, all your classmates agree,
you'll bring home the trophy and win the spelling bee."

"Our school has never won although we've tried and tried."
All the kids began to cheer to show they were on his side.

Big Zeke felt overwhelmed and didn't know what to say.
He thought about it but the fear simply wouldn't go away.

"I can do this, I'll practice night and day
and I won't let anything get in my way."

Although his friends would stop by
to ask Big Zeke to come out and play
he would say, "No thanks, not today."

He continued to study and practice,
with his head stuck in a book.
Determined to do whatever it took!

As the Regional Spelling Bee began,
everything went according to plan.

At first Big Zeke easily won round after round,
as his class cheered him on with a thunderous sound.

The words got harder as the day moved along,
and then his fear of losing became very strong.
This was a feeling he knew he could not allow,
as the sweat started to drip down from his brow.

The last word was announced
and it was a difficult word indeed
but all of Big Zeke's work paid off
with a Spelling Bee Victory.

He took home the trophy
and brought his school a win.
The word he spelled correctly was
"Self-Discipline."

NO FISH TODAY
#10 Accurate Thinking

When the school bell rang at the
    end of the day,
Oliver watched as the older boys
    passed his way.

As usual they were heading to
    their fishing spot,
all the way at the end of the
    abandoned lot.

The lot was dense and full of trees.
You couldn't even see beyond the
    leaves.
Oliver wondered what they *really* did out there.

"We are going fishing," the older boys would say,
but no poles or fish were seen day after day.

Kids looking on let their imaginations take flight
and instantly replied with their own insight.

"They go into the woods to set large fires.
No matter what they say, they're all big liars.
They sneak into coops and steal chicken eggs.
They even capture frogs and bite off their legs."

Oliver said, "No that can't be,
I'll find out for myself just wait and see."

Oliver followed the boys the very next day
making sure he stayed far, far away.

He watched them go through the dense trees,
in some spots even crawling on their knees.

It was hard to keep up but Oliver wanted to know.
As the journey went on his curiosity started to grow.

They reached a clearing at the end of the lot,
finally arriving at their fishing spot.

Much to Oliver's surprise
there were the poles waiting inside
a small boat they boys called 'Pride.'

Oliver was happy when he saw what came next,
they released each fish they caught in their net.

He watched as the boys laughed and had fun
and couldn't wait to tell everyone...

Sometimes things aren't what they seem.
These boys were fishing,
fishing indeed!

THE MUSIC IN ME
#11 Controlled Attention

Olivia's class was going to see a
   Special Musical Play
but she had little to no interest in
   going that day.

The musical began and she couldn't
   have been more wrong,
she was standing and clapping
   and singing along.

That night Olivia lost sleep tossing
   and turning in bed,
she simply couldn't get the music
   out of her head.

Morning came and she couldn't wait to get to school
to speak to her Band Director Mrs. O'Toole.

Olivia talked on and on about the Special Musical Play
and how her greatest desire was to have a solo one day.

"It'll take hard work I already know
but I really want my very own Solo."

"I'll make the commitment and stop playing around
once I get focused I'll create the best sound."

Mrs. O'Toole replied with glee,
"I'm glad you are finally taking it more seriously.

I've always known the clarinet was perfect for you,
now apply yourself and show me what you can do."

Olivia happily brought home her clarinet
to learn a lesson she would not soon forget.

She pulled it out excited to play a musical tune
but to her surprise it wouldn't happen too soon.

She realized she needed to learn the notes.
Especially how to hold the clarinet right,
and this certainly would not happen overnight.

Olivia continued to practice day after day,
knowing hard work and dedication bring a solo her way.

The night of the school play had finally arrived
and Olivia's level of practice could not be denied.
She took center stage and played with all her might
as everyone clapped and cheered in sheer delight!

Her heart's desire to play had finally come true
and you can find the music in you!

TEA PARTY MADNESS
#12 Teamwork

Olivia was sitting in her room one day
remembering the tradition
her Grandma passed her way.

Throwing Tea Parties made Grandma DeDe
the talk of the town
bringing people together from all around.

To have an experience like no other
and Olivia wanted to be
just like her grandmother.

Continuing this tradition
and showing her friends something new,
Olivia decided she wanted
to throw a Tea Party too.

"Elegance and glitz is what it will be.
Mother can I please throw a Tea Party?"
"That would be wonderful!" her mother agreed.

"Mom I'm so excited to work as a team
to turn this into my Tea Party Dream!
I'll invite Annabel, Kayla and Juliet too.
Monet, Mia, and Mya and the Malone twins,
just to name a few."

Baking for the big day began
as Olivia and her Mother worked their Tea Party plan.

With their hands covered in batter and dough,
the amount of cookies started to grow.

Olivia and her mother cheerfully sang,
when the front doorbell suddenly rang.

As they both turned around without missing a beat,
their little dog Cody snuck in for a treat.

He jumped on the counter and made quite a mess,
turning her Tea Party Dream into Tea Party Madness.

His paw hit the pan and dough flew
   in the air
and teacups came crashing down
   everywhere.

Olivia turned back and let out an
   enormous scream,
"PLEASE STOP HIM Mother, he's
   ruining everything!"

There was a big sticky mess on the
   floor
as her friend Kayla walked through the door.

"Don't worry my dear we'll put Cody outside
and we'll get everything together,"
her mother calmly replied.

Kayla chimed in, "I will help you too,
that is what a good friend would do."

They cleaned up the mess as quick as could be
and continued to prepare for the Tea Party.

Sandwiches were cut into small bites
as they baked up new cookie delights.

The house filled with the smell of fresh brewed tea
as her friends started arriving for the Tea Party.

Mother, Olivia and Kayla made a great team,
turning Tea Party Madness into a Tea Party Dream.

FROM ASHES TO BLACK GOLD
#13 Learning From Adversity & Defeat

Oliver, Olivia and Big Zeke were
    getting off the bus
as Mother sat quietly waiting with
    news to discuss.

They walked to the door and
    stopped at the steps.
Something bad happened and it
    was quite complex.
Mother sadly shared, "Our biggest
    fear has come true
and your father and I are deciding
    what to do."

"One thing after another has not gone our way
now the family barn burned to the ground today.
But you don't have to worry the animals are okay."

"So much has gone wrong since we moved to this town,
it's time to pick up and find some new ground."

The kids were in disbelief from what they heard
and the thought of leaving was truly absurd.

Olivia pleaded, "You taught us not to run away
even when things aren't going our way.
We can make it through even though it's bad.
Please don't make us leave, let's talk to dad."

Oliver and Big Zeke eagerly agreed too,
they needed a better plan for what to do.

"We don't even mind selling all of our toys,
we'd rather stay here, it would bring us more joy.
All of our friends at our school will help too.
Let's rebuild the barn and start anew."

Overwhelmed by the kids response that day,
it touched Mother's heart in a positive way.
So she talked to their dad and decided to stay.

Mother reached out to her book club friends,
while neighboring farmers began pitching in.

More hands made the work load light.
To get the job done they worked day and night.

They realized the joy they found in this town
and were glad they decided to stick around.

When they got down to the last bit of soil,
you wouldn't believe it...the family Struck Oil!

They jumped and shouted with all their might.
They hit it big and life changed overnight.

What a valuable lesson they learned that day,
that sometimes life's little blessings
come in the most mysterious way.

Who would have thought the Hill family
would go from Ashes to Black Gold?
This is the grandest story ever told!

JULIE'S SPECIAL RECIPE
#14 Creative Vision

Months have passed since the county fair
where Julie, Joe, and Oliver's ice cream flavor
won with no compare.

The townspeople continued to ask day after day
for them to create new flavors to send their way.

Since Julie loved making things that were sweet,
she thought, "Why not, this could be such a treat."

Her eyes got bigger as her vision became clear,
"I can start an Ice Cream Business later this year!"

She thought of the wonderful flavors she could create
and how the townspeople would line up at her gate.

Idea after idea came into her head
as her imagination was fed.

"New flavors fashioned after Grandma's recipes
that could be my very own specialty."

Julie couldn't wait to call Oliver and tell him the news.
She picked up the phone and started to dial
and got more excited as they chatted a while.

After hearing her ideas, Oliver readily agreed
a Summer Ice Cream Business would surely succeed.

Too bad Joe couldn't participate.
He spent summers away with his Great Uncle Nate.

Although the trio was now down to two
this was a task this pair could do.

Off to work Julie and Oliver began
creatively making a business plan.

The sky was the limit they couldn't deny
the townspeople would gladly buy buy buy!

Julie jotted down recipes she learned long ago.
Sweet treats like Blueberry Muffin Cookie Dough
and Chewy Cherry Pie in a big Donut Hole...

Triple Chocolate Fudge with Whip Cream on top.
With all these amazing flavors no one would stop
eating more ice cream day after day
and sending more townspeople their way.

And with so many spectacular flavors to choose
their imagination grew and their business did too.
Making Julie's Creative Vision a dream come true!

HAPPY TEETH
#15 Maintenance of Sound Health

Oliver enjoyed all of his tasty ice
  cream treats,
day and night he would eat eat eat.

Until one day his tooth felt very sore,
it was something he could not ignore.

He dreamt the dentist pulled all his
  teeth out
so he woke up in a sweat and began
  to shout!

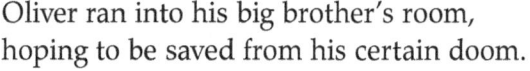

Oliver ran into his big brother's room,
hoping to be saved from his certain doom.

"I don't want to lose my teeth
from all the sweets stuck underneath."

Big Zeke half asleep laughed in Oliver's face,
"Stop being a baby. It's not as bad as you think.
Not all of your teeth will end up in Dr. Green's sink."

"I really wish you would stop waking me up,
you are worse than Cody, our pup."

Oliver regretted not brushing his teeth
as well as he knew he should
and would do it differently if he could.

Around the breakfast table that morning
as the family ate bacon, eggs, and toast,
Oliver could only eat jello at most.

His mother sensing that something wasn't right,
asked Oliver why he hadn't taken a bite.

Finally Oliver decided to come clean
even though he didn't want to go see Dr. Green.

"Mom, I've been in so much pain,
my teeth are driving me insane.
But I'm scared to get them all pulled out,
please help me before I scream and shout!"

"Oh dear, I'm sure it won't be that bad,
we'll go see the dentist, trust me you'll be glad."

To Dr. Green's office they went and he was redeemed.
It wasn't anything like Oliver had dreamed.
All he needed was to get his teeth cleaned.

Not brushing his teeth was something he couldn't hide.
The soreness was caused by the sprinkles stuck inside.

He said he'd learned his lesson that day,
on the importance of brushing the proper way.

Oliver burst into his new *Happy Teeth Song*
and he encourages you to now sing along:

*"It's fun to brush my teeth each and every day,
brushing up and down keeps cavities away.
Two minutes in the morning and two minutes at night,
brushing them daily keeps them nice and bright.
Now my teeth are happy and yours can be too.
I'm glad Dr. Green showed us what to do!"*

PAY YOURSELF FIRST
#16 Budgeting Time & Money

Big Zeke was looking up at the sky
as planes raced and flew really high.

In an instant they would flip upside down
and loop and loop and loop all around.

Big Zeke and his dad enjoyed the High Flyer Show.
They were so glad they decided to go.

After the High Flyer Show came to an end,
into the gift shop Big Zeke went to spend spend spend.

He picked up everything from model planes
to goggles, even t-shirts and a pen!
Paying no attention to cost,
his shopping had no end.

Once his arms were overflowing with things to buy,
he walked up to the register and stepped aside.
Looking to his dad to buy it all, but his dad replied,
"Nice try! Where's your money to buy all of this, Son,
you get a weekly allowance and now you have none???"

Big Zeke said, "I have no idea where my money goes.
As soon as I get a dollar in my hand
it slips through my fingers like grains of sand.
I can't help but spend it, isn't that what you do?"

"No, Son. There is a lesson I want to share with you,
a lesson that will last your whole life through.
Big Zeke this is something I wish I learned as a child,"
said Dad, wrapping his arm around him as he smiled.

"You never want to spend more money than you earn.
Pay Yourself First, is the lesson you must learn."

"Set aside at least 10% or more if you can.
Here son, let me help you to understand.
Out of every single dollar you make,
listen carefully, Son, ten cents is yours to take
and put aside to save and grow for you."

"At first glance this may seem like a small amount
but over time it can become humongous and count.
You'll be able to do whatever you want to do
including buying model planes, even real ones too!"

Big Zeke got excited and began to understand
that saving his money was the perfect plan.

He decided today was the best day to start.
Paying himself first would play a big part
in helping him get the money he would need
to bring about his wildest dreams indeed.

His dad allowed him to pick one item from the bunch
that he'd treat him to along with his favorite lunch.
Big Zeke picked the model plane he saw in the show
as a symbol of how he would make his money grow.

Big Zeke hugged his dad with all
    of his might,
as he knew his future would be
    very, very bright!

LIVING OUT LOUD
#17 Cosmic HabitForce/Universal Law

Big Zeke stumbled upon a secret door
well hidden in the family's basement floor.
He ran to his room with the contents in hand
telling Oliver and Olivia to meet him as planned.

"I found these two envelopes covered in dust
which said only open around those you trust."
Oliver ready to see what Big Zeke found
sat quietly next to Olivia on the ground.

He opened the envelope labelled *Penalties You Pay*.
It listed bad habits you must avoid each day:
*"Being lazy and stubborn and drifting through life
ungrateful and jealous and full of much strife."*

*"These are things that will bring lots of pain.
Avoid these as you'll have nothing to gain."*

Olivia chimed in, "I don't like that list!
I want a life filled with happiness and bliss."
Big Zeke and Oliver readily agreed,
"Let's open the other envelope and read."

The second envelope labelled *Rewards You Gain*
contained a list that wouldn't cause pain:

"Decide what you want and follow through,
have faith and courage and love what you do.
Just as the sun goes up it must come down.
What you give you get, it all comes back around.
The riches of life will be yours to take
and the life you live is yours to make."

Big Zeke and Oliver stared off into space
and Olivia sat quietly trying to embrace,
the words they read certainly gave them a chill.
It was signed, *"All the best to you,* Grandpa Hill."

"I think I finally got it," Oliver said with pride.
"The more good I do, the more happiness I keep.
When I form good habits, it's rewards that I'll reap!"

Big Zeke and Olivia said, "Yes, that's it!
Living that way we'll be happier, you must admit.
Let's get started today and make Grandpa proud
by forming good habits and living out loud!!!"

Conclusion

We hope you enjoyed coming along for the ride
and allowing Olivia, Big Zeke and I be your guide.
Now it's your turn to learn from these lessons too,
as situations arise you'll know exactly what to do.
Please be sure to keep this amazing book close to you.
If you want to make your wildest dreams come true,
reading from it daily will give you a clear view.
Make sure you stay in touch, there's so much more to do.
Life is full of amazing adventures and success that awaits you!

                                        Your Friend,
                                              Oliver

List of Suggested Children's Books by Principle

Principle #1 - DEFINITENESS OF PURPOSE
1. *What is My Song?* Written by Dennis Linn, Sheila Fabricant Linn, & Matthew Linn SJ. Paulist Press. 2005.
2. *Follow the Moon.* Written by Sarah Weeks. Illustrated by Suzanne Duranceau. HarperCollins Publishers. New York. 1995.
3. *The Tale of Three Trees.* Retold by Angela Elwell Hunt. Illustrated by Tim Jonke. Kingsway Communications. England. 1989.

Principle #2 - THE MASTERMIND ALLIANCE
4. *Stone Soup.* Jon J. Muth. Scholastic Press. 2003.
5. *The Little Red Hen.* The Talking Mother Goose Series. Retold by Margaret Huges. Worlds of Wonder. 1986.
6. *The Classic Treasury of Aesop's Fables.* Illustrated by Don Daly. Running Press. 1999. Pg. 47.

Principle #3 - APPLIED FAITH
7. *The Trellis and the Seed.* Jan Karon. Penguin. 2003.
8. *Leo the Late Bloomer.* Robert Kraus. Pictures by Jose Aruego. Windmill Books. New York. 1971.
9. *The Velveteen Rabbit.* Written by Margery Williams. Illustrated by Don Daily. Courage Books. Philadelphia, PA. 1997.

Principle #4 - GOING THE EXTRA MILE
10. *The Dandelion Seed.* Written by Joseph Anthony. Illustrated by Cris Arbo. Dawn Publications. Nevada City, California. 1997.
11. *The Giving Tree.* Written and illustrated by Shel Silverstein. HarperCollins Publishers. New York. 1992.
12. *The Carrot Seed.* Written by Ruth Krauss. Illustrated by Crockett Johnson. HarperCollins Publishers. New York. 1973.

Principle #5 - PLEASING PERSONALITY
13. *Buttons.* Written by Tom Robinson and illustrated by Peggy Bacon. Penguin. New York. 1991.
14. *The Jolly Postman* by Janet and Allan Ahlberg. Tien Wah Press. Malaysia. 2001.
15. *Pete the Sheep-Sheep* by Jackie French and illustrated by Bruce Whatley. Clarion Books. New York. 2004.

Principle #6 - PERSONAL INITIATIVE

16. *Brother Wolf of Gubbio.* Written and illustrated by Colony Elliott Santangelo. Handprint Books. New York. 2000.
17. *Jam & Jelly* by Holly and Nellie. Written by Gloria Whelan. Illustrated by Gijsbert van Frankenhuyzen. Sleeping Bear Press. Chelsea, Michigan. 2002.
18. *Angelina Ballerina.* Katharine Holabird. Illustrated by Helen Craig. Pleasant Company Publications. Middleton, Wisconsin. 2000.

Principle #7 - POSITIVE MENTAL ATTITUDE

19. *The Little Engine That Could!* Retold by Watty Piper. Illustrated by George & Doris Hauman. Platt & Munk Publishers. New York. 1976.
20. *The Frog Prince* by Brothers Grimm. Grimm's Fairy Tales. Diversion Books. New York. 2015.
21. *Aladdin & The Magic Lamp.* Written by John Patience. Once Upon a Storytime Series. 1988.

Principle #8 - ENTHUSIASM

22. *How I Became a Pirate.* Written by Melinda Long. Illustrated by David Shannon. Harcourt, Inc. Mexico. 2003.
23. *The Secret Remedy Book:* A Story of Comfort and Love. Karin Cates and Wendy Anderson Halperin. Orchard Books. 2003.
24. *Granddad's Fishing Buddy.* Written by Mary Quigley. Illustrated by Stephane Jorisch. Penguin. New York. 2007.

Principle #9 - SELF-DISCIPLINE

25. *The Quilt Maker's Gift.* Written by Jeff Brumbeau. Illustrated by Gail de Marcken. Scholastic Press. New York. 2001.
26. *Daniel O'Rourke: An Irish Tale.* Written by Gerald McDermott. Puffin Books. Penguin. New York. 1986.
27. *The Dance.* Written by Richard Paul Evans. Illustrated by Jonathan Linton. Simon and Schuster. New York. 1999.

Principle #10 - ACCURATE THINKING

28. *Seven Blind Mice.* Written by Ed Young. Philomel Books. New York, New York. 1992.
29. *The Fisherman & His Wife.* Written by The Brothers Grimm. Illustrated by John Howe. 1983.
30. *The True Story of the Three Little Pigs!* Written by John Scieszka. Illustrated by Lane Smith. Puffin Books. Penguin. New York. 1989.

Principle #11 - CONTROLLED ATTENTION
31. *The Three Questions.* Written and illustrated by Jon J. Muth. Scholastic Press. New York. 2002.
32. *A Small Child's Book of Prayers.* Collected and Illustrated by Cyndy Szekeres. Scholastic Press. New York. 2002.
33. *The Itsy Bitsy Spider.* Told and illustrated by Iza Trapani. Whispering Coyote Press. Dallas, Texas. 1993.

Principle #12 - TEAMWORK
34. *Together...We can.* Written by Beth Shoshan and Petra Brown. Paragon. United Kingdom. 2012.
35. *Don Quixote and Sancho Panza.* Adapted by Margaret Hodges. Illustrated by Stephen Marchesi. Charles Scribner's Sons Books for Young Readers. New York. 1992.
36. *Meet the Orchestra.* Written by Ann Hayes. Illustrated by Karmen Thompson. Harcourt. New York. 1991.

Principle #13 - LEARNING FROM ADVERSITY & DEFEAT
37. *Tear Soup.* Written by Pat Schwiebert and Chuck DeKlyen. Illustrated by Taylor Bills. Grief Watch. Portland, Oregon. 2004.
38. *I'm Sorry.* Sam McBratney. Illustrations by Jennifer Eachus. HarperCollins Publishers Ltd. 2000.
39. *Alexander and the Terrible, Horrible, No Good, Very Bad Day.* Written by Judith Viorst. Illustrated by Ray Cruz. Aladdin Paperbacks. Division of Simon and Schuster. 1972.

Principle #14 - CREATIVE VISION
40. *What Do You Do With An Idea?* Written by Kobi Yamada. Illustrated by Mae Besom. Compendium, Inc. Seattle, WA. 2013.
41. *Roxaboxen.* Written by Alice McLerran. Illustrated by Barbara Cooney. Lothrop, Lee & Shepard Books. New York. 1991.
42. *Where The Wild Things Are.* Written and illustrated by Maurice Sendak. Harper Collins. 1991.

Principle #15 - MAINTENANCE OF SOUND HEALTH
43. *Waiting for Benjamin.* A Story about Autism. Written by Alexandra Jessup Altman. Illustrated by Susan Keeter. Albert Whitman & Company. Illinois. 2008.
44. *Me, Stressed Out?* Written and illustrated by Charles Schulz. Harper Collins. 1996.
45. *What's Happening to Grandpa?* Written by Maria Shriver. Illustrated by Sandra Speidel. Little, Brown and Company and Warner Books. New York. 2004.

Principle #16 - BUDGETING TIME & MONEY

46. *The Busy Beaver.* Written and illustrated by Nicholas Oldland. Kids Can Press, Ltd. Ontario, Canada. 2011.
47. *No Room for Napoleon.* Written by Adria Meserve. Random House. New York. 2006.
48. *What Time Is It, Mr. Crocodile?* Written by Judy Sierra. Illustrated by Doug Cushman. Harcourt, Inc. New York. 2004.

Principle #17 - COSMIC HABITFORCE

49. *All I See Is Part Of Me.* Written by Chara M. Curtis. Illustrated by Cynthia Aldrich. Illumination Arts. Washington. 1994.
50. *Old Turtle.* Written by Douglas Wood. Watercolors by Cheng-Khee Chee. Scholastic Press. New York. 1992.
51. *Sofia's Dream.* Written by Land Wilson. Illustrated by Sue Cornelison. Little Pickle Press LLC. California. 2010.

52. *Winnie the Pooh.* Written by A. A. Milne. Penguin Group. New York. 2009.

Works Cited by Napoleon Hill

1. *Think and Grow Rich.* Random House. Trade Edition. 1996. Pgs. 37-38.
2. *You Can Work Your Own Miracles.* Random House. 1996. Pgs. 75-76.
3. *Grow Rich with Peace of Mind.* Random House. 1996. Pg. 128.
4. *Succeed and Grow Rich Through Persuasion.* The Napoleon Hill Foundation. Penguin Books. 1991. Pgs. 167-168.
5. *Succeed and Grow Rich Through Persuasion.* The Napoleon Hill Foundation. Penguin Books. 1991. Pgs. 79-80.
6. *PMA Science of Success.* Educational Edition. The Napoleon Hill Foundation. 1983. Pgs. 73-74.
7. *PMA Science of Success.* Educational Edition. The Napoleon Hill Foundation. 1983, Pgs. 83-84.
8. *You Can Work Your Own Miracles.* Random House. 1996. Pg. 81.
9. *PMA Science of Success Course.* Educational Edition. The Napoleon Hill Foundation. 1983. Pgs. 87-89.
10. *PMA Science of Success Course.* Educational Edition. The Napoleon Hill Foundation. 1983. Pg. 121.
11. *Grow Rich With Peace of Mind.* Random House. 1996. Pgs. 31-32.
12. *How To Sell Your Way Through Life.* The Napoleon Hill Foundation. 2005. Pgs. 152-153.
13. *PMA Science of Success.* Educational Edition. The Napoleon Hill Foundation. 1983. Pg. 163.
14. *Succeed and Grow Rich Through Persuasion.* Penguin. 1992. Pgs. 154-155.
15. *PMA Science of Success Course.* Educational Edition. The Napoleon Hill Foundation. 1983. Pgs. 195-196.
16. *PMA Science of Success Course.* Educational Edition. The Napoleon Hill Foundation. 1983. Pgs. 206-207.
17. *Think and Grow Rich* A Ballantine Book, Published by Random House Publishing Group 1960. Pgs 210-211.
18. *Law of Success in Sixteen Lessons.* The Original Unedited Edition. Volume II. The Napoleon Hill Foundation. 2013. Pgs. 8-9.
19. *PMA Science of Success Course.* Educational Edition. The Napoleon Hill Foundation. 1983. Pg. 231.
20. *Success Through A Positive Mental Attitude.* Prentice-Hall, Inc. 1960. Pgs. 24-25.

21. *Success Through A Positive Mental Attitude.* Napoleon Hill & W. Clement Stone. Prentice-Hall, Inc. 1960. Pgs. 234-235.
22. *PMA Science of Success.* Educational Edition. The Napoleon Hill Foundation. 1983. Pg. 250.
23. *Napoleon Hill's Magazine.* July, 1921, Pg. 23.
24. *Success Through A Positive Mental Attitude.* Napoleon Hill and W. Clement Stone. Prentice-Hall, Inc. 1960. Pg. 121.
25. *PMA Science of Success.* Educational Edition. The Napoleon Hill Foundation. 1981. Pgs. 269-270.
26. *PMA Science of Success.* Educational Edition. 1983. The Napoleon Hill Foundation. Pgs. 268-269.
27. *PMA Science of Success.* Educational Edition. 1983. The Napoleon Hill Foundation. Pgs. 286-287.
28. *Success Through A Positive Mental Attitude.* Napoleon Hill & W. Clement Stone. Prentice-Hall, Inc. New Jersey. 1960. Pgs. 35-36.
29. *Think and Grow Rich.* Ballantine Books. Random House. New York. 1983. Pgs. 120-121.
30. *Think and Grow Rich.* Ballantine Books. Random House. New York. 1983. Pg. 121.
31. *PMA Science of Success.* Educational Edition. The Napoleon Hill Foundation. 1983. Pgs. 331-332.
32. *Grow Rich With Peace of Mind.* Ballantine Books. New York. 1996. Pgs. 45-46.
33. *PMA Science of Success Course.* Educational Edition. The Napoleon Hill Foundation. 1983. Pgs. 333-334.
34. *PMA Science of Success Course.* Educational Edition. The Napoleon Hill Foundation. 1983. Pgs. 355 & 356.
35. *PMA Science of Success Course.* Educational Edition. The Napoleon Hill Foundation. 1983. Pgs. 361 & 362.
36. *PMA Science of Success Course.* Educational Edition. The Napoleon Hill Foundation. 1983. Pgs. 373 -374.
37. *Grow Rich! With Peace of Mind.* Ballantine Books. Trade Edition. 1996. Pg. 21.
38. *Think and Grow Rich.* Ballantine Books. 1983. Pg. 221.
39. *PMA Science of Success.* Educational Edition. The Napoleon Hill Foundation. 1983. Pgs. 395-396.
40. *PMA Science of Success.* Educational Edition. The Napoleon Hill Foundation. 1983. Pg. 401.
41. *Law of Success in Sixteen Lessons.* The Original Unedited Edition. Volume II. The Napoleon Hill Foundation. 2013. Pg. 70.
42. *Think and Grow Rich.* Ballantine Books. 1983. Pgs. 72-73.
43. *PMA Science of Success.* Educational Edition. The Napoleon Hill Foundation. 1983. Pgs. 425-426.

44. *You Can Work Your Own Miracles.* Fawcett. 1971. Pgs. 48-49.
45. *Grow Rich With Peace of Mind.* Ballantine Books Trade Edition. 1996.
46. *PMA Science of Success.* Educational Edition. The Napoleon Hill Foundation. 1983. Pgs. 459-460.
47. *You Can Work Your Own Miracles.* Napoleon Hill. Fawcett Gold Medal Books. New York. 1971. Pgs. 130-131.
48. *PMA Science of Success.* Educational Edition. The Napoleon Hill Foundation. 1983. Pgs. 481-482.
49. *Grow Rich! With Peace of Mind.* Ballantine Books. New York. 1996. Pgs. 231-232.
50. *You Can Work Your Own Miracles.* Fawcett Gold Medal Books. New York. 1971. Pg. 120.
51. *Think and Grow Rich.* Ballantine Books. New York. 1983. Pg. 194.

For additional information about Napoleon Hill products please contact the following locations:

Napoleon Hill World Learning Center
Purdue University Calumet
2300 173rd Street
Hammond, IN 46323-2094

Judith Williamson, Director
Uriel "Chino" Martinez, Assistant/Graphic Designer

Telephone: 219-989-3173 or 219-989-3166
email: nhf@purduecal.edu

Napoleon Hill Foundation
University of Virginia–Wise
College Relations Apt. C
1 College Avenue
Wise, VA 24293

Don Green, Executive Director
Annedia Sturgill, Executive Assistant

Telephone: 276-328-6700
email: napoleonhill@uvawise.edu

Website: www.naphill.org

www.ingramcontent.com/pod-product-compliance
Lightning Source LLC
LaVergne TN
LVHW011415080426
835512LV00005B/69